Victory

DENISE HYLTON

Victory
Copyright ©2025 Denise Hylton

ISBN 978-1506-915-40-1 PBK

October 2025

Published and Distributed by
First Edition Design Publishing, Inc.
P.O. Box 17646, Sarasota, FL 34276-3217
www.firsteditiondesignpublishing.com

ALL RIGHTS RESERVED. No part of this book publication may be reproduced, stored in a retrieval system, or transmitted in any form or by any means — electronic, mechanical, photocopy, recording, or any other — except brief quotation in reviews, without the prior permission of the author or publisher.

Disclosure
This book is based on a true story. To protect privacy, I have changed the names and details of the people. While these events happened as I described them, certain facts have been altered.

I dedicate this book to everyone who identifies or seeks encouragement, resulting from your own personal struggles. This story will provide inspiration that will spark the strength and tenacity needed to attain victory in the midst of life's overwhelming challenges.

May you experience true victory in life's journey.

VICTORY

"Success is not measured by what you accomplish, but by the opposition you have encountered, and the courage with which you have maintained the struggle against overwhelming odds."

Orison Swett Marden

FOREWORD

Victory, is a riveting tale of an innocent young girl's journey from trials to triumph. Genise lost her mother at the tender age of six years' old! This exposed her to the horrors and harsh realities of life.

Having to endure superstitions, occultic practices, betrayal, racism and a myriad of emotional and psychological abuse that would have challenged her for many years.

Joy became elusive and happiness was always fleeting, as life became a constant cycle of challenges.

Join the captivating journey of an innocent young girl as she navigates childhood trauma on route to attaining, lasting victory.

Weeping may ensure for a night but joy comes in the morning!

Mrs. Carline Wint- Mattison
Administrator, Government of Jamaica.

INTRODUCTION

Genise with all expectation of having parents around to provide that sense of stability – love, security and a happy home. But in an unexpected turn of events- the sudden death of her mother (Betty). Genise along with her two younger siblings were sent to live with their grandparents in St. Elizabeth. Grandma affectionately called Icy or Mama had strange occultic, cultural beliefs and practices that were seemingly passed down to her from her fore parents. She believed that the "Spirit of Betty"- her first of her four daughters who had died mysteriously leaving Genise and her siblings ages two, four and six would return and take her children to the grave to be with her. Hence, it was her responsibility to "guard", Betty's Dead Left Pickney Them" – (*The name given to Genise and her siblings after the death of their mother*).

Grandma believed that the Witch doctor/*Obeah-man* could protect her grandchildren and the members of her family from untimely deaths and from daily evil attacks.

These practices weaved the values and belief systems that were taught to Genise, her siblings, cousins and the rest of her maternal side of family. Genise and all her (motherless) cousins were raised by their grandmother in St. Elizabeth during their formative years.

Grandma loved Genise and her siblings dearly, but she did not see the need to take Genise and her siblings to church to ensure that they were christened, blessed or even to let the church pray for their protection.

Instead, grandma protected the children by "anointing" them with the strange ointments and vials that she bought from the Obeah man.

However, unknown to Grandma the poignant vials, lotions, ointments and concoctions that she used to "anoint" the children daily to protect them; would create mysterious happenings resulting from the evil altars that were erected each time she took vials from the Obeah man. (This led to dire consequences for her and her lineage). And would affect both her children's and grandchildren's lives for generations to come.

As in a dramatic turn of event instead of protection for the family the opposite seemingly took place: grandma lost all her four daughters, they all died mysteriously and in rapid succession of each other. Leaving behind children between the ages of two to six years old. she had to endure the crushing pain of burying her daughters who all died before the age of forty years old. She also had to care for her motherless grandchildren.

Being without the protection, support and coverage of a mother, Genise had to exercise and cultivate great tenacity and courage to overcome constant abuse, racism, evil altars, witchcraft activities, abandonment, rejection, hurt, financial hardships, the untimely death of her mom and other unexplainable mishaps throughout her early years. But God intervened by raising up Genise the only Christian from Icy's lineage and empowered her with the wisdom and understanding to *"stand in the gap"* through prayer and repentance as she cried out to God for His forgiveness on behalf of herself and her family: with a view to prevent the destruction of the entire lineage as she denounced and reverse the evil covenants and altars that were erected. Genise then replaced these evil altars (covenants that were made with the *Obeah man*, occultism, witchcraft etc.) with righteous altars by choosing life: (via *salvation through the blood of Jesus Christ as an antidote for her sin and the sins of her fore parents*).

Genise also resolved in her heart to pray and fast, determined to break free from every bondage, curse, and hardship. She made a deliberate choice to embrace life, standing firmly on the truth of God's word, which declares:

"I call heaven and earth to record this day against you, that I have set before you life and death, blessing and cursing: therefore choose life, that both thou and thy seed may live." — **Deuteronomy 30:19**

CHAPTER 1

THE GENESIS

Children are a gift from the Lord; they are a reward from him.
                              ~ **Psalm 127:3**

Ruptured ripe mangoes and guavas on the ground released an overpowering tropical fragrance that permeated the air. Stones unforgiving to bare feet littered a narrow dirt track that led to a small board house tucked away from prying eyes in a plethora of fruit trees. In the backyard, a burbling stream leaped for joy over weathered rocks and glinted as the sun's rays greeted its surface.

The occupants of the house were 18-year-old Betty Hutton and 31-year-old Lester Hill – a love-struck couple. They never missed a moment to glue their lips together and melt into each other's arms. Every Friday night, the Kingston Waterfront was their dance floor as they rocked and swirled at Bob Marley's "Is This Love."

"The vendors are looking at us Les," Betty said as she rubbed her nose against his.

"I didn't even notice them," Lester replied. "Let them enjoy the show."

After their performance, roasted corn and red peas soup was always a wholesome treat as they watched the moon drift across the sky. The night seemed endless whenever they were together, and so was their love.

Betty a comely woman with soft curly hair that was always restrained by a scarf. Hints of European ancestry showed in her blue-green eyes that accentuated her caramel skin. Some may have found her too reserved, but she exuded an undeniable warmth around dear friends and family. If the neighborhood grapevine were a class, she would have gotten an award for perfect absence. Even though her education never went beyond All Age School, she was the most brilliant of her three sisters; her parents always trusted her to conduct business on behalf of her family.

Lester was dark-skinned, short, and slender. His long thick black dreadlocks, bushy eyebrows, and dark lips from years of smoking gave him a serious look. He was a boisterous man and very passionate about every topic, which made him an excellent conversationalist. Whenever he wins a game of domino with friends, you could hear his roar of laughter from miles. A welder by profession, he spent sunrise to sunset on weekdays working to appease his clients' requests no matter how elaborate they were. He had spent years perfecting his craft while building a solid client base in the hope of supporting a large family which was his dream.

He had met Betty in downtown Kingston while she was purchasing a stove for her parents. Her meek appearance arrested Lester's attention, who hypnotized her with his raspy voice and flirtatious comments. This first encounter was the

Victory

beginning of many others with young and impressionable Betty, it was not long before Betty found herself in a relationship with Lester. She fell in love with him and eventually ran away from her home in St. Elizabeth to live with her newfound lover in St. Catherine.

The stove she bought was never delivered to her parents' house but instead had found refuge in her new home with Lester.

Somehow, Lester and Betty managed to live harmoniously with the termites that nibbled at the very existence of their home and the roaches that had made their base under the kitchen sink. The aroma of burnt orange peels made mosquitoes uncommon in the house. There were old shoes stuffed with cardboard, moth-eaten curtains, were patched and doilies were thrown over worn furniture – nothing was thrown away. They did not have much, but they had each other, and that was all that mattered.

One day, Betty dashed through the dense bushes screaming at the top of her lungs, "George! George! Come back here!" Her foot caught a branch that had fallen from an almond tree, and she stumbled forward, but Lester managed to grab her before she could hit the ground.

"Are you trying to kill yourself?" Lester asked. "George is dead, remember?"

Betty wept bitterly as she hugged Lester. "I know; I know" she said "But I just saw him" as she clung even tighter to Lester.

Memories of her blood-soaked frock electrocuted her mind, and the pain of that fateful day butchered her heart once more. Unfortunately, there was no pain medication for her emotional wounds. Time appeared to be mocking her rather than helping her to heal. Her tears and Lester's embrace brought temporary relief to her heavy heart before the hauntings resumed. Permanent peace, day by day became elusive.

Lester tried to comfort her as they walked back to the house arm in arm. He gave her a cup of strong ganja tea, and some calloo and fried plantain in a calabash to soothe her.

He burnt incense to rid the tension in the atmosphere and put her mind at ease. When a neighbor had suggested counseling for him and Betty, Lester abruptly ended the conversation asserting that it was a scam. Though he was not a man to wear his emotions on his shirt, Lester was still hurting too, but he had found comfort in smoking ganja as often as he could to quiet his nerves, and he kept himself busy. Gushing tears would wreak across his face hidden by the splashes of water from the river where he customarily had his bath."

Tears were only allowed to escape during bath time when the river water would mask them as he washed his face.

Betty and Lester were in separable they consoled each other and so they decided to try for another child.

The months sped quickly by and soon Betty became pregnant and gave birth to their love child Genise. Baby Genise brought a bit of fresh air and joy to their home. One day halfway through her meal Betty looked at the clock, and realized that Genise, their daughter, was still asleep.

She had been in a kind of drunken stupor over the past three days and showed no sign of being fully alert.

The belly rubs and tickles on her tiny feet proved futile in waking her. She was warm and still breathing, however Betty was deeply concerned about her condition. She snatched her handbag and commanded Lester to quickly take them to the hospital. She gently grabbed the baby while Lester gathered a few items they would need and immediately rushed out behind her.

Victory

As they raced with their daughter to the nearest hospital, thoughts of George, their firstborn love-child ran through Betty's mind which brought on a deep sense of sadness as she sat silently in the taxi next to Lester. George died under a different circumstance. Genise was only six months old and could not possibly suffer the same fate.

Within a few minutes they had arrived at the hospital which was already overcrowded with patients. They rushed to get the child registered and assessed and were given a number to wait until they were called to see the doctor.

While waiting for what seemed to be a considerable length of time, Betty and Lester spoke in soft tones to each other. The area where they were sitting was teeming with people all with many different com-plaints.

The area in which they sat was filled with different sights and sounds. Laughter could be heard coming from a section where a group of men sat talking. In another corner a young girl was heard crying as she held and rubbed her tummy. The sound of ambulances arriving filled the air and created a symphony of sounds and emotions.

Number 75! a voice rang out over the loud speaker. "That's us", Betty responded. They got up swiftly and were directed to the doctor's office by the nurse at the desk.

As they entered the office they were greeted by a tall, handsome looking doctor who invited them to take a seat. Betty cuddled Genise in her arms while Lester sat close to her with his arm around her waist.

The doctor asked about what had happened to the child to which Betty responded with some degree of uncertainty, however, she stated that the child was not acting as normal as she was constantly sleeping throughout the day.

After giving the doctor, a list of all the food Betty had eaten over the past few days, Lester's mind drifted to the day of George's death. He had finished welding a client's barbeque grill when he heard Betty's ear-splitting screams. He flew into the house, almost breaking down the door, and was greeted by Betty covered in blood lying on the floor. Her face told a heartbreaking story of distress.

His reflection was interrupted by a sudden thought of the ganja tea he had given to Betty all week. The doctor's phone rang and as he went out of the room to take the call Lester used the opportunity to lean into Betty and whispered, "remember the ganja tea I gave you?"

"Yes," she said with eyes planted on her daughter. "It probably converted to breast milk and that's why the baby is sleepy," he mumbled. Betty, with her eyes wide open, softly replied, "Ganja is illegal in Jamaica, and they'll send us to jail if the doctor finds out." As Betty uttered these words, they both got up and hurriedly left the hospital with their daughter."

Lester mixed an antidote of sugar and water into a strong syrup as soon as they got home and gave Genise to drink. A sigh of relief came when Lester pinched Genise to awaken her, she began to cry screaming at the top of her lungs, Betty began to play with her daughter and quieted her, a few minutes later; she opened her eyes and began to look around with a puzzled look on her face. Betty and Lester vowed to keep this event a secret to their graves. Not even their closest family members would ever know.

Five years had elapsed since the passing of baby George and the birth of Genise. Genise was the firstborn of Betty's two other children since George's death.

Betty would often beam with a smile whenever she looked at her children. She was grateful that God had allowed her to experience that chapter in her life called motherhood, no matter how short it was. In the depths of her dark brown eyes;

Victory

however, was a constant sadness brought about by memories of one of their love child, George.

CHAPTER 2

THE BREAKING POINT

The Lord is close to the brokenhearted and saves those who are crushed in spirit.
~Psalm 34:18

One Saturday morning in September 1986, Betty crisscrossed downtown Kingston, gathering food and household supplies for her family. While walking along the street, she heard someone call her name but could not locate the person in the thick of the crowd. "I haven't seen you since George died," said a familiar voice. She turned frantically into circles in a sea of people trying to locate the person. The hair on her skin stood at attention; she breathed heavily as her heart pounded and her muscles began to stiffen.

It felt as if her feet were glue to the ground. Then she felt someone grab her arm from behind.

"Getaway!" shrieked Betty. Then, as she pulled her arm away, she realized that it was her sister, Beatrice.

"You look like you've seen a ghost. Good heavens!" Beatrice remarked. "You know I'm not the witch that beguiled George, right? If you keep thinking about what happened, surely it will send you to your grave too."

"Good, then see you at my funeral," Betty snapped as she stopped her sister from embracing her. "You need to stop this bad behavior; it's like you're a different person whenever someone mentions George. I guess that's why you don't visit mama and papa often anymore because you know they'll bring it up."

"Kiss my nieces and nephews and tell them I love them."

"You know I had a bad dream about you last night. I dreamt that ..." but before Beatrice could finish the sentence Betty interrupted, "stop pestering me!"

The two sisters stared intensely at each other with fists clenched and poised as if ready to begin round one of a boxing match. Those standing around were arrested by the commotion between the two sisters and they looked on with much anticipation of the debacle being played out before them.

Suddenly Betty stormed off and hurriedly made her way to the taxi stand. She just wanted to go home. It had been five years since George her first-born son had died, but any mention of his name still tore her heart to pieces. Although she had three other children, a part of her would always be missing. It is a loss that only a few can understand.

Suddenly, she felt a slap on the back of her neck. She turned around in a split second to unleash her fury on the perpetrator, but saw no one. There were only a few people at the taxi stand, and none within immediate reach of her.

As she stood there pondering what had just happened, an unexpected dizziness suddenly came upon her. The bags in her hands began to sway from side to side, while the ground seemed to fade beneath her feet.

A taxi driver standing nearby and looking on noticed her distress and quickly reached out to her, concerned that she might fall to the ground. He asked her if she was ok and if she need a taxi. She responded yes and told him where she was going. He then helped her into his vehicle and immediately sped off like he was being chased by arm thugs.

By the time the taxi arrived at her home she was too weak to get out of the car by herself. Betty was drooping like a withered plant and could only muster up enough strength to say, "Get me Lester, I feel like I am going to die."

Lester and the taxi driver quickly lifted her from the vehicle and carried her inside the house. By this time, a few of the neighbors had gathered around the house with quizzical looks on their faces.

"Nothing that a little ganja tea can't cure," he reassured himself. "Mama, mama!" her children screamed in a chorus as they ran towards her. Lester with a wave of his hand quietened them down while he reached over to where he stored his ganja.

But like a streak of bad luck, Lester realized that he somehow had run out. He thought to himself maybe he had used it all when he hosted his friends for an exciting game of dominoes the night before. The small brown jar which kept the smelling salt did not even have a single grain inside, and his herbal plants were still just seedlings in the ground. With one hand on his head, he paced around the house while rummaging through every container looking for some type of remedy he could give to her. Lester stood there pondering what to do next.

"Boss man you running out of time!" said the neighbor. Looking over at her, Lester noticed how pale she had become;

Victory

deeply concerned he decided to take her to the hospital which was only a few miles away. He called out to a nearby passing taxi to assist them.

Help me get her into the car, Lester shouted as he lifted her from the bed. After placing her on the back seat, Lester said, "I am going to call another neighbor to keep the children while we are gone."

As the taxi drove off, Lester glanced back and saw the neighbors in the distance struggling to hold on to the children as they wailed and cried out for their mother. Finally, Genise managed to break free and tried running after the taxi with tears streaming down her face. Unfortunately, her sprint ended abruptly when she fell headlong, sustaining cuts and bruises to her elbows and knees.

"Quick! Quick! driver go faster," Lester bellowed. He began to curse and hissed his teeth in his impatience to get to the hospital.

Lester started to reflect once more. He remembered the thin layer of fat resembling a mesh-like merino that had covered George when he was born. During Betty's pregnancy, doctors were unable to detect the presence of a fetus and instead thought that she had excess fat in her womb. However, when it was finally discovered that she was in fact pregnant doctors concluded it was a cryptic pregnancy.

This incident was the second time death was knocking on his family's door. He thought to himself that two is a charm, and Betty would come home to the children.

Upon arrival at the hospital, Betty's skin had gotten paler, and she was barely uttering any words. Then, before they even made it into the emergency section, she collapsed in Lester's arms taking her final breath. Lester slouched against a tree on the hospital compound. They were only a few feet from the emergency ward.

Lester let out a loud wail as he cuddled his beloved Betty in his arms. He held her just as he had held George when he died.

"Jah Jah! Jah Jah! why she and not me?" he howled. His howls were so loud that the birds retreated from their mid-afternoon snack in the fruit trees.

Medical personnel were summoned as curious onlookers stared and expressed their sympathy. She was just 24 years old. Betty's death was a devastating blow for Lester and his children. He was a man almost defeated. First George, then Betty, the grief was more than he could bear.

He could not even gather himself to arrange the funeral, it had to be done by Beatrice.

After the funeral, Betty's parents took the children to St. Elizabeth to live with them. Lester had asked for some time to be alone to grieve and to heal and promised to come for the children as soon as he could. They were aged, six, four, and two.

Genise the eldest of the children, was traumatized by her mother's sudden death and would wait in vain every day hoping to see her mother appear. Grief swelled the atmosphere. Everyone thought Betty had finally found true solace in death, but no one dared to say that.

CHAPTER 3

DEAD LEFT PICKNEY DEM

From the end of the earth will I cry unto thee, when my heart is overwhelmed: lead me to the rock that is higher than I.
                                              ~Psalms 61:2

Genise and her siblings were called, "The Dead Left Pickney Them" after the death of their Mother. They were taken to St. Elizabeth to live. Genise's grandfather grew sugar cane on several acres of land in St. Elizabeth which he sold to sugar companies. He also raised goats, cows, and pigs on ten acres of land all of which he had inherited from his father. From the sale of sugar cane and livestock, he was able to secure large profits which he used to provide his family with a comfortable life.

Genise's grandfather was not one who wore his emotions on his sleeves. He was a private person and did not speak much. After Betty's passing, he would go out very early in the mornings and returned late in the evenings to avoid his neighbors who may wish to converse with him about Betty's death. He became withdrawn and he began to have less interactions with the members of his family. He did not talk much after his daughter's death and refuted any claim of a duppy [*ghost*] cutting short her life.

Being quite a superstitious community, many persons believed that a ghost had slapped Betty on the back of her neck, causing her mysterious and untimely death. This sentiment was strongly shared by Betty's mother, Icilinda Hayles, affectionately called Icy "mama, grandma " and "granny."

Icy was a firm believer in witchcraft and the afterlife. Her deep African roots where witchcraft was practiced as a religion motivated many of her actions. She believed the witch doctor or "Obeah man" could explain life's mysteries and help her to escape from any pitfall that may stand in her way. It was her method of weathering life's storms, and she believed that the dead could be communicated with and thus sought the advice of dead relatives via the witch doctor.

If a drinking glass broke, she believed it was caused by evil spirits and would visit the witch doctor to obtain protection. She had several books on witchcraft and would go to the back of the house at midnight to perform strange rituals. Her obsession with the dark arts was unfettered and she devoted many hours of her time to her quest to gain as much knowledge as she could to feel empowered and to control her destiny. She was as the proverbial scholar seeking mastery yet interestingly; she could not even spell witchcraft or words above a few letters.

"Betty got pregnant at the early age of 16," said Icy with arms crossed. "Foolish gal, to have made friends with a witch because, I rebuked her about her pregnancy. George born and died shortly after his birth, and now the ole Jezebel finish her off."

"She had it coming," a neighbor replied.

Unlike her husband, Icy never shied away from engaging the neighbors about her daughter's death. She deeply regretted not supporting her daughter when she was pregnant, but believed George had to die due to the covenant the witch had made with the evil spirits after Betty had taken George to her. Everything happens in the spiritual realm before the physical realm. With this knowledge, Icy believed that it was her responsibility to protect her grandchildren from all evil. She thought that the children's dead mother would return from the grave, kill them and take them. As a result, she would go to the witch doctor, who would give her some strange, pungent-smelling liquid in vials to rub on the children daily.

Icy would have the children do some strange things too. For example, she would get dreams and visions from Betty who would tell her which schools the children should attend. She also instructed the children to frequently visit their mother's grave to say hello and speak with her. She even told them that she once saw their mother under a cotton tree near the house.

"Your mother said that she is upset with how your stepmother is always hitting all three of you," said Icy as she pounded the table with her fist. "Your stepmother is nothing but an evil spirit."

"Old woman, you're talking nonsense," Lester said as he entered the room laughing uncontrollably. "Their mother is dead, and the same bible you read said spare not the rod and spoil the child."

"But Papa, beating always set my bottom on fire," said Genise.

"Excuse me, miss, you're in adult conversation now, and that's why you must get beating," said Lester as he pointed her to the door.

Regardless of their grandmother, Lester's girlfriend religiously spanked his children whenever she visited. Even the slightest laughter would evoke hellfire wrath that she would unleased upon the children. Truthfully, any mother, dead or alive, would have been upset. Lester's girlfriend mysteriously did not return after finding grey liquid with burnt paper in her bag one night. It was believed by many to be one of Icy's concoctions to get rid of her, and even if it was not Icy's doing, the plan worked.

Strange things always happened, and Icy's explanation would continuously be, "it is your mother who is responsible." Icy ensured they never forgot their mother. Although she was dead, she still had a hand in how she raised them.

One morning when Genise woke up, she found that someone had cut up all the clothes in the closet. Of course, Icy said that the culprit was Betty. These mysterious experiences and Icy's constant communication with the children's dead mother weaved the story of the lives of Genise and her siblings in St. Elizabeth.

"I catch you," her grandmother said. "All if you run go bush, I would find you."

Genise would always try to hide whenever she saw granny coming with the vials. She could not endure another baptism of strange liquids. But as soon as she thought she had escaped, she would be caught, placed in bath and lathered with a concoction of mysterious liquids. And finally with carbolic soap that made her nauseated.

The water from the hose masked Genise's tears as her grandmother washed off the soap. She thought of different ways to escape the ritual, but she knew that grandma would still find a way to do it even if she was asleep. Genise believed that the constant nightmares and wrestling with evil forces were because of these rituals. Unfortunately, the teddy bears were no source of comfort to her, and she lived her life in constant fear.

To make matters worse by the time Genise had gotten to the age of twelve, all her grandmother's daughters mysteriously died within the next six years. It appeared the family was under a generational curse. First, all Genise's aunts including her mother all got pregnant in their teenage years, and now all of them were dead.

Icy may have managed to protect herself and her two sons from evil spirits, however her four daughters were less fortunate. They all died, leaving behind young children whose age ranges from 2 to 6 years old.

Icy stood at her gate lamenting about the death of her daughters as she recounted what the Obeah woman had told her concerning their deaths.

Her second daughter was killed because of money, the third one had a best friend who became jealous of her relationship with a man that she wanted for herself, so she got rid of her. The fourth daughter was killed by someone who had ill feelings towards her.

The postman who was delivery mail on hearing her story commented "I will pray for you."

"I don't need prayer. I need vengeance," Icy said, rubbing her chin. As a result, Icy continued to make more frequent visits to the witch doctor for advice and instructions. which she used to perform a long list of rituals.

The witch doctor enriching herself from Icy's frequent visits was able to travel to Miami for a lavish vacation – she never returned she had made enough money from Icy.

The neighbors who previously had shown much interest in engaging Icy in conversations about Betty's death now kept their distance when her three sisters died in rapid succession. It was not long before they started referring to the motherless children as "the dead left pickney them."

The death of the children's mothers caused great heartache and pain for all Icy's grandchildren. They were left to navigate their teenage years without their mothers. This also affected Genise and her siblings, who suffered bitterly at the hands of an abusive stepmother and caretakers.

The witchcraft world may have been a place of healing for Icy, but in contrast it cast an aura of death, sadness and darkness in the family home.

The family later realized that instead of protecting Icy and her children, the witchcraft rituals and practices did just the opposite.

It took Genise years for her to experience any form of normalcy in her life; the generational curse had to be broken. Once she realized that the strange practices of her grandmother had invoked "evil altars", thus resulting in curses upon her family, she was able to break-free from the evil altars and generational curses through forgiveness, confession of her sins and surrendering her life to Jesus Christ.

CHAPTER 4

KINGSTON

To everything there is a season, and a time to every purpose under the heaven...
                                        ~Ecclesiastics 3:1

It was mid-afternoon when Lester and Genise arrived at their destination. The place looked strange, but the beauty of the house caught her attention. Something was different, how did their little board house transform into a royal castle? When did the narrow dirt road become a wide asphalt road? Why were the neighboring houses so close?

These questions pricked Genise's mind, and her inquiring eyes roved the surroundings. She cautiously stepped out of the vehicle for a more detailed look and quickly concluded that this was not the home she knew as a child.

A young woman strolled down the brightly colored corridor towards the gate. She looked no more than 27 years of age. As she came closer, Genise noticed a large scar across her chest that looked like it came from a chop wound. Even more noticeable was her provocative attire which left very little for the imagination.

She wore a closely fitting dress and her large boobs which juggled for space were just about ready to pop out to the delight of the men passing by. Her smile revealed several crooked teeth and a missing canine.

"Ah boy, you certainly don't look like my type," Lester said.

"No worries. You are paying me to take care of the kids, not you," she said with a wry smile on her face. "By the way, welcome to Kingston!"

"Stop frightening the poor children with your loudmouth, and let's get them settled", Lester replied.

A short tour of the property revealed well-manicured lawns. The dwelling itself was one of grandeur depicted by its exquisite architecture and overlays. On the inside of the dwelling, the most beautiful pieces of handcrafted furniture could be seen. Mahogany furniture with gold trimmings could rival the latest arrivals at brand name furniture stores.

Lester's hands ran through the satin curtains, and its soft touch was a warm greeting to his fingertips. "My father built this house, and I inherited it when he died,". "Now it's up to me to make it into the home it needs to be," said Lester.

"Why didn't you live here before now?" the young woman asked.

"I'm a simple man. Nothing too fancy for me, but I want my children to have what I never had when I was a child," replied Lester.

"I don't even feel I can manage on my own, especially with girls. I don't know the first step in taking care of them."

"A good father can take care of his children regardless of their gender," the woman replied.

She turned to the children and said, "By the way I am Tamara. My pa is a friend of your dad, and I'll be taking care of you for a while."

Genise's eyes lowered, and a feeling of sadness washed over her. She was eleven (11) years old and had spent most of her life without a mother, and now she was going to spend more time away from her father. She already did not have a close relationship with her siblings, but she thought anything was better than living with her grandparents.

Lester nudged Tamara on the elbow and indicated to her to follow him to another room while the children were left playing on the floor. Lester handed her a brown envelope. "Now, at the end of every week, I'll look for the children and bring groceries," he said. "This money can serve for two weeks, so make it last because you see that it is me alone with them."

"Where is my share?" Tamara said with raised eyebrows. "Don't tell me you can't afford to pay me, but you can buy fancy furniture for the house."

"Stop worrying yourself; I'll pay you at the month-end."

"Good."

With her hand firmly placed on Lester's back, she ushered him out of the house without Odetta and Dean noticing. "Daddy," Genise screamed. "I'll be back soon Genise, just behave yourself and remember your manners," Lester replied before exiting the premises.

5-year-old Dean realized too late that "daddy" was gone and wrapped himself in the curtain as he wailed.

When he refused to unwrap himself, Tamara grabbed the hot iron from the ironing board so that he could feel the heat. The heat lured him out, but his weeping persisted.

"What are you crying for, boy?" Tamara barked. "If you don't stop crying, this heat is not leaving you."

Dean probably wished he had listened when Tamara pressed the iron down on his belly, swallowing all the skin on its surface. Odetta screamed like she was losing her mind and sought refuge in the linen closet. Genise took a big gulp, her eyes wide open, filled with tears and lips parted – maybe living with her grandmother was better.

"If any of you tell your father about this, I will put you all out, and you will have no one to care for you," she said with disgust. "And don't stress me out either; I don't have the time for people hard ears pickney."

It was the trailer for the horror movie that would unfold gradually. Tamara barely fed the children and would tease them with pieces of food before eating them. Tamara confiscated snacks brought by their father, and she would give a proper beating to anyone who managed to capture any portion of food without her permission.

The refrigerator was full, but the children's stomachs were empty. Hunger pains and water became familiar friends to the Hutton's children over the years. Sometimes they resorted to receiving meals from their friends' lunch pans at school or picking up fallen fruit as they walked home.

Unfortunately, after long periods of hunger, they could not keep food in their bodies, and vomiting became another constant in their lives. One night, Genise rushed to the hospital for urgent care because she was too weak to stand. Lester never knew about the harsh treatment of his children because they were fearful of being homeless.

The situation was unbearable, and Genise spent many nights sobbing. She was not experiencing nightmares anymore because she was living them. She did not have the luxury of being kissed and told bedtime stories at night like her other friends. No one to comfort her when she skinned her knees, no one to appreciate her artwork done at school, and no one to teach her how to navigate a changing body when her period made its first appearance.

Genise's search for love seemed hopeless. The only time she felt something close to peace was whenever Tamara would go out on Friday evenings.

Tamara always allocated all the money Lester sent for the children for personal spending. As a result, the children had the same clothes month after month, while Tamara bought a new item every week. Even more disturbing, she programmed the children to look like they were doing well when their father came, so he did not suspect any abuse. They were more than happy to see their father because it was the only time they were usually given a proper meal, sometimes too much food, and a sound bath for the youngest.

After one of Lester's visits, Genise told Tamara she was hot and wanted a cool glass of milk. "Go milk your fingers, little girl," Tamara growled. "If you want to feel cool, sit in front of the fan with wet clothes, and it will feel like A/C." Genise did precisely that and suffered from a terrible cold that rattled her chest whenever she coughed. Leaf of Life plant that was used to make cold medicine proved to be useless in fighting the month-long cold, and she eventually had to see a doctor that diagnosed her with bronchial pneumonia. The neighbors spoke on occasions to Lester about Genise's condition; however, Tamara informed him that his daughter had played in the rain, disobeying her orders.

Tamara was very convincing, the subtleness in her voice played on Lester, and he believed her every word. Genise's slightest objection to what had truly transpired, resulted in her teddy bear being beheaded.

Genise's spirit was crushed and inside of her she felt hollow. Countless times, she had packed her bags to run away, but she felt too beaten and defeated to muster the courage to do so. Now would have been the ideal time for her dead mother to punish Tamara. The searing pain of her broken heart became the only thing that reminded her that she was alive.

There were no birthday parties, no buns and cheese at Easter, and no fruitcake at Christmas. The atmosphere at the house forbade any type of celebration. There were no games, no playing, and no watching television. It was like they were in an eternal holding cell of constant torment by the devil's henchwoman.

Every night, she wished that the death angel would whisk her away to be with her mother forever. Her thoughts were interrupted by memories of her asking family members for pictures of her mother. She had only a vague memory of what her mother looked like. Icy and Lester told her that Betty never liked taking pictures. Therefore, no photographs of her were around – it was as if she never existed.

"How can I miss someone that I never really knew?" Genise sobbed. "I wish there was someone who loved me."

The stars were her bedtime story, sadness tucked her in, and her tears put her to sleep.

Chapter 5

THE ATTACK

Many are the afflictions of the righteous: But the LORD delivereth him out of them all.
                              ~Psalm 34:13

The next day was lovely. The afternoon sun was up, yellowing the land. The lawns were green; new buds had grown on the trees. The walk to her house from school was peaceful. However, as soon as Genise got closer to her gate. Tamara approached her.

"Hurry up! change your uniform and go and buy rice for dinner!" Tamara bellowed.

Genise slipped into a loosely draped orange T Shirt, sparking an imaginary security feature of a blanket covering her shorts and her slender ninety-pound frame beneath.

"Can I have the money to buy the rice?" Genise asked.
"Here!" Tamara replied.

Tamara angrily slapped the money on the dark wooden table at the side of the door and stormed out of the kitchen.

Genise, face drooped like a wilted plant as she dragged her feet and reluctantly scrambled towards the door. Outside, there was no wind. The bright sun beamed down and heated the pavement on the sidewalk. Genise could feel the heat beneath her feet as she gingerly walked to the shop. Suddenly and without warning, she heard a loud, horrible snarling sound coming close to her. What she then saw increased the thumping of her heart.

She screamed, "oh no!" in panic as a "dark object" raced towards her. She froze. Fear and terror gripped her heart as she quickened her pace. She tried to run but could not coordinate her limbs. The ground underneath her felt uneven. She stumbled. Then the enormous dark hairy object pounced at her, throwing the weight of its body on her slender ninety-pound frame. She fell backward onto the ground.

Her cries for help were desperate, high-pitched and piercing. She screamed for her life causing the birds in the nearby trees to flutter away from their resting position.

The next few seconds unfolded in what seemed like a terrifying scene from a horror movie as her ear-splitting screams filled the atmosphere. It was a ferocious wolf-like dog that had attacked her as it ferociously bites at her face. With upheld hands, she tried to ward off the humongous beast but, in the process, the dog had gripped her hands in its vice-grip-like jaws.

As she struggled to free her hands, the dog suddenly let go but this time lounging at her neck. It was a vicious attack on her. Genise cried out in terror. Her desperate plea for help caught the attention of some men who were working at a nearby garage.

They grabbed whatever they could and ran towards the dog to hopefully break its grip from off terrified Genise and save her from what would have been a fatal tragedy. After striking the dog several times, the men somehow managed to get the dog away. There was silence for a moment as the men looked at her frame lying on the ground. She was bruised, battered and torn. The dog had ripped away some of her clothing, exposing her body and several teeth mark could be seen.

Suddenly and to their amazement Genise got up from the ground. She was very shaken but possessed enough strength to stand on her own.

The men who had come to her rescue tried their best to console her and assisted her in locating her money that had been scattered on the ground during the attack. That was to be used to buy rice.

Finally, the men asked her for directions to her house. She was still trembling and sobbing. Genise managed to point in the direction of her home, which was only a few meters away.

A few minutes later, a troubled man in a scruffy looking uniform arrived at the scene. His eyes appeared half-closed; he seemed confused and noticeably tired; his movements were faltering as if each step pained him. He dropped his head as he looked at the ground. It was as if he was breathing without really being alive. In his hand was a broken leash. He began to plead with the men and small group of passersby who were now at the scene.

He profusely apologized for the unfortunate accident. He blamed his colleague, who did not show up to relieve him from his shift. He explained that he had worked the overnight shift and had merely dozed off. Then in a split second, he realized that the dog had broken the leash and had escaped and thus carried out the attack.

Beyond the issue of criminal liability of his carelessness lies the more profound puzzle that seems beyond his illogical explanation of the event.

The men and the passersby surrounding the scene were furious. The security guard was very confused and troubled. One of the men almost ripped off his head. The men grabbed him to beat and execute him. It nearly turned into a "jungle justice" situation.

He gave his credentials as he identified himself; he also gave the men the address and contact number for his company. He was very sorry for what had happened and promised that he would ensure that Genise was compensated for the terrible accident.

He explained that his organization trained the dog. He further pointed out that even though the dogs' training includes rag-biting techniques, they were obedient to the guards.

The security guard noted that the dogs usually respond well if you try to restrain them and never attack children.

It was the longest Journey Genise had ever taken to her house. Her heart, feet, and limbs would not coordinate as she felt the pain of the dog's bites and bruises on her body, which burnt like pepper. The men accompanied Genise to her gate. They knocked and banged on the gate so hard that even a few neighbors were seen looking out while Tamara came running to the gate.

As she approached the entrance, she saw the men standing at the gate. Her heart raced as if she was about to have a heart attack. What is this? She thought as her mind entered as state of panic when she saw Genise knowing that Lester would surely kill her.

The men told Tamara what had happened. Tamara's eyes bulged from their sockets; a crazed look covered her face.

Victory

"WHA"! "WHAT"! Tamara's voice stammered with-fear and concern. A rush of adrenaline made it hard for her to think. Her body shook with anger as she gripped the gate until her knuckles turned pale as if all the blood had drained from them. The men put their arms around her as they tried to calm her down.

The men gave her the name and contact information that they have received from the security guard. They told her to take Genise to the doctor to ensure that she was not infected with rabies from the dog's bite. Tamara, still in shock by the incident, straight away rushed Genise to the hospital. The dog bite had broken into her skin and was swollen. The doctor gave Genise an injection to prevent the possibility of rabies infection. Exhausted, Genise went to bed early, finding solace in the embrace of sleep. Lester arrived for the weekend and heard of the ordeal. He was almost defeated and decided to take his children to live with him at his home in St. Catherine. The security guard never made contact.

CHAPTER 6

THE RETURN

And I will restore to you the years that the locust hath eaten....
~ **Joel 2:25**

The alarm clock sounded at 6.30 a.m. Genise opened her eyes, wiggled her toes, and moved her legs. "Oh nooooo! It's Monday morning!" realizing that she had overslept; At once, she flew out of bed stripped down and jumped into the shower. Minutes later, she dashed out of the bathroom: dressed, snatched a sandwich, and, in a desperate hurry, ran across the street just in time to catch the school bus that arrived promptly at 7.30 a.m.

The move to St. Catherine was a huge struggle. Genise no longer walked to school. She now had to wake up early to catch the school bus. Although it was difficult at first, eventually, she adjusted. Still, there was a stir of excitement in Genise's heart. It was a new beginning, a new season, and a new lifestyle.

Victory

The children rocked sideways as the school bus turned the corner and neared the main road at the end of the narrow dusty road.

Genise's mind drifted as she reminisced on how swiftly her five (5) years at Rousseau Primary School had zipped past and that she was now sixteen (16) Years old.

Moreover, she had seen the end of her childhood and was now in the middle of her teenage years as she journeyed into adulthood. She reflected on her past friends and teachers in 4th grade. One teacher in particular, Mr. Coote, was an exceptional literature teacher who made the sacrifice to encourage and mentor her; he made learning fun and left an indelible mark on her life.

Not all Genise's memories were pleasant, that "*wicked witch*" Miss J'africa Devine, who taught English Literature, how could she forget her, once Genise asked her a question to which she replied, 'weren't you listening? I just answered that!' Genise rarely asked her any questions or spoke in her class after that."

As soon as she neared the schoolyard, her daydreaming abruptly ended when she heard a faint sound, "Genise, did you pass?" bellowed Harry as he ran with glee towards the door. She removed the cotton swab that she had forgotten in her ears, and replied, "WHAT WHAA?"

"It's exam results day!" shouted Harry.

'That's impossible," Genise replied.

Genise felt as if a lightning bolt had hit her. She felt a surge through her veins; her heart pounded, her skin tingled, her body quivered. For a moment, she found herself in an electrified state. Suddenly the school bell rang; it was time for general assembly.

To her surprise, the principal called her name.

"Genise Hutton. Come to the podium."

Genise was successful in her exams! And had earned a place at Ardenne High School, one of the most prestigious high schools in Kingston!

A prolonged rapturous applause could be heard from the student body and teachers as the entire school celebrated all the children who were successful in their Common Entrance Examination. The rest of the day was filled, with excitement and was marvelous.

As soon as the school bus reached the gate to her house, Genise could see that the sun was setting, casting the sky in a brilliant array of oranges, whites, and purples. The scene reminded her of a multi-colored rose that she once received and cherished dearly as a child. Genise had always loved to watch the sunset.

Lester had gotten the newspaper earlier that day, so he and all the neighbors knew that Genise had successfully passed her exams.

As Genise stepped off the school bus, Lester and the neighbors were very excited to see Genise and greeted her; they were all excited, they hugged and tightly squeezed Betty's dead left pickney!

Lester was very proud of his daughter's achievement and felt as if he had received a surprise gift. Lester knew that his transition into the role of a single parent had been very challenging. His children did not have the same access to full parental support as many of their friends. This made it difficult for his children to cope; it was very daunting for them and for him.

For the first time, however, he felt a glimmer of hope in his heart, gently assuring him that he was on the right path. He must now chart the course of life for himself and his family.

Victory

No matter how ridiculous it may feel at times, it was like asking a fish to climb a tree. Finally, God had smiled down on him. His hard work had paid off. With a teary-eye, Lester managed to smile when he remembered Betty the love of his life. He felt sorry that she was not alive to take part in the celebration. Later that night, when the children were asleep, Lester reclined in his chair on the verandah and let the happiness soak right into his bones. He wanted the feeling to linger. He closed his eyes and savored the moment but never released his grip on the seemingly inconsequential piece of newspaper in his hands. For the first time in forever, his body and mind relaxed. At that moment, there were no expectations upon him, no deadlines, and no schedules to meet. He had set a foundation for his daughter; despite the trauma, he was victorious, and he felt like a winner.

Chapter 7

THE GIFT

Every good gift and every perfect gift is from above, and cometh down from the Father of Lights, with whom is no variableness, neither shadow of turning.

~James 1:17

The news of Genise's success spread in her community and caught the attention of Margret Elsa Myers, a well-spoken caucasian woman with a very friendly voice who lived nearby.

Margret congratulated Lester and as a "*gift*" to Lester, she offered to take Genise to live with her and promised to financially take care of Genise's high school education and to support her by welcoming her into her loving family home.

Lester accepted the gift; he felt as if it was a perfect gift from a fellow parent who saw and understood his struggles as a single father with three children. He spoke with Genise regarding the offer made by Mrs. Myers, and she was ecstatic about it.

Genise always looked forward to Mrs. Myers taking back that delicious chocolate from Switzerland her native home. Mrs. Myers married a Jamaican. Each summer she would return to the place of her birth and Genise could not wait for her return to get her special package. How creamy and sweet those chocolates tasted. She could never have enough; and now she was being told the exciting news that Mrs. Myers would be taking her into her home and would treat her as one of her own children.

Finally, Genise would get the "*mother*" she had longed for, who would help her navigate the challenges of her adolescence years as her body went through the various changes into womanhood. Little did Genise knew that her excitement would dramatically evaporate, as life became a balance of wonderland and nightmare!

The first thing Margret did upon Genise's arrival to her house was to tell her that she would have to be transferred from the prominent high school in which she was placed for her successes in her exams; And that she would have to go to the same school that all her sons attended.

If she refused, she would have to go back to her dad who was not in the position to adequately provide for her and give her life's luxuries.

Margret did this behind Genise dad's back and would constantly nag Genise to tell her dad that she wanted a transfer. Genise was weary and although heartbroken eventually succumbed to the pressure.

Margret constantly warned her not to tell her dad and convinced her to tell her dad that she wanted a transfer to a school nearby! Genise's sister Odetta also stayed with Margret for a brief period. One day, Margret made a prune pie. Odetta, who was not feeling well, had eaten enough when she refused to eat the rest of the prune pie Margret was livid and slapped her in the face. Odetta began to cry and as she cried Margret began to force the food down her throat, suddenly Odetta started vomiting.

Margret furiously commanded her to eat the vomit and when Odetta refused, she took the vomit, rubbed it all over her face, and then locked her into a dark room as punishment for her disobedience. Margret knew that Odetta was afraid of the dark, but this did not faze her.

Odetta was traumatized and cried all night until she had no tears left.

Margret had three mixed race sons who were all much older than Genise.

Genise normally sits beside one of her sons at the dinner table in the evenings. One evening Margret said to one of her sons, "Genise loves sitting next to you in the evening for dinner".

Her son replied, "well, at least I do not have to look at her."

Margret would allow her sons at times to speak condescendingly to Genise and would do nothing to correct them!

Also, Margret would sit in front of Genise and discuss Lester and her siblings with her friends. She would lie to them by telling them that Lester had begged her to take Genise to help him, because he was unable to take care of his children! She would laugh with her friends telling them that Genise and her family lived in an "*ants' nest*"!

Whenever Genise's friends would call her via the telephone or visit her at home. Margret would shout at them and tell them not to call or visit Genise at her house again, because Genise was a foster child in her home.

And if they called again, she would threaten to complain to the school and their parents. She would also tell them that they had the wrong number and that no one lived there by that name.

Margret and her sons would do this in Genise presence in the most condescending way, without any regards for Genise's feelings or emotions, nor did she consider the fact that her friends would laugh or whisper about her in school the next day.

Life at Margret's house was likened to that of a boot camp. Genise had a list of duties that must be done each evening, and if they were not done, she would be slapped in the face. Margret had a blackboard where she wrote and counted any careless errors that Genise had made and would update and calculate these daily. If she made many errors, all her pocket money that she had gotten would be taken away from her.

In the evening at a certain time Margret would turn off all the lights and Genise would have to carry out the rest of her chores that must be done in the dark, which includes combing her hair!

At times Genise would feel sad in her spirit, when she realized that the yearning that she felt on the inside for a mother's love was constantly being crushed. Although there was always enough to eat and a clean bed to sleep in, Margret showed Genise no love, no respect or attention.

Margret also helped a little boy named Patrick; Patrick's mother was insane and had given birth to him on the street. An old woman took him up and grew him as her son. As this old lady got older, she could no longer take care of Patrick, so Margret offered to take care of him also.

Patrick was 8 years old, and whenever he could not remember his Bible verse, Margret would take the big study bible and while he was asleep would hit him in his head. This would cause him to fall off the chair and crashing to the floor where he would scream and cry out, she would also give the handy man a strap and ask him to beat him because he was much stronger than she was and could hold him firmly and beat him with the strength of a grown man.

The handy man would beat Patrick mercilessly, life with Margret was far worst for Patrick than it was for Genise because Patrick had no real family! At least Genise had her siblings and her dad!

One night as Genise was at the dining table she decided to write a letter to her friend in Canada telling her how Margret had been treating her and Patrick and how she was so disappointed that her dad had sent her to live with Margret.

Genise's letter made Margret furious. She took the letter and threatened to send it to all of her schoolteachers, the principal, her dad and even the newspaper if she talked to anyone about the way she treated her and Patrick.

Genise spoke to her second form teacher about it who told her that Margret was a white witch, who was intent on destroying her, and told her to be careful of her!

Genise left school that day and when she arrived home, she asked Margret to send her home to live with her dad. Margret was embarrassed, and worried that the letter that Genise had written would be exposed to others, so in a desperate attempt to salvage her reputation.

Margret threatened and blackmailed Genise with the letter. Threatening to publish Genise's letter in the newspaper and to send to the principal of the school. Genise did not want to hurt or embarrassed her father, so she agreed to let Margret keep the letter and in return Margaret allowed her to return and lived with her dad.

Margret was so manipulative that she also warned and black mailed Genise and told her that she should not discuss with her dad anything that happened at her house and that if she disobeyed her warning, she would also give copies of the letter that she had written to her friends to her dad and his friends. Genise only agreed to Margaret's threats because she had denounced her dad's poor and foolish decision to allow her to live with Margaret who was a very deceptive and manipulative individual, in her letter to her friend in Canada, and as a direct result of this Genise did not want to hurt or disappoint her dad who like her had been clearly beguiled and deceived by Margaret. Genise knew in her heart that her dad had worked very hard over the years to take care of her and her siblings after the death of their mother. As a result, she did not want to crush his spirit so she never told her dad of the constant threats or abuse that were meted out to her by Margret.

Her myriads of bad experiences she and Odetta had to endure from living with Margret's weaved the devastating stories of emotional, racism, psychological and verbal abuse and created invisible wounds that ran deep within Genise's heart, soul and mind.

Lester's children experienced harsh ways of life and as they grew older, they understood that no one in the world would love them the way their dad did, or their mother would have if she was alive. The true love that they yearned for was elusive at best and instead Genise suffered at the hands of a very deceptive Narcissist (Margret).

CHAPTER 8

THE SECRET

For his anger endure but a moment; in his favor is life: weeping may endure for a night, but joy cometh in the morning.

~**Psalm 30:5**

"Daddy, I'll be back soon," said Genise patting her father's shoulder.

"Where are you going?" asked Lester.

"I am on my way to church." replied Genise. "Then why are you carrying your school bag?" asked Lester.

Genise smiled and said "Daddy, I am getting baptized this evening, so I have to carry a full change of clothes."

Lester laughed hysterically and signaled to his friends to pause their game of domino. "Guess what? My big daughter said that she is going to church to get baptized tonight!" Again, the men burst into laughter.

Victory

The smile disappeared from Genise's face as she stared at them in disbelief. However, she was adamant that their mockery would not stop her from being baptized. Finally, she had found a home, a family – in the church. Her heart's deepest desires finally came to fruition, and no one would take that away from her, not even her father. She slowly walked down the pathway fighting the tears in her eyes.

Genise was almost at the entrance of the church when she saw her dad riding his bicycle towards her. She walked faster, kicking up a storm of dust beneath her feet, but he caught up with her just as she entered the churchyard.

"Genise, are you getting baptized tonight?" he said.

"Yes, daddy," she said with her face turned away from him.

He pointed his finger at her face. "Genise, what are you doing? Are you getting baptized to worship the white man's God?" "Yes."

"I am warning you, don't do it! Don't let me reach the yard before you," he barked.

A small crowd gathered to witness the meltdown. Some felt pity; others giggled. Lester stood still; the look he gave his daughter was sharp enough to cut through wood. She knew that he was serious and narrow streams of saltwater flowed from her eyes. A fellow church member ushered her into the church, and Lester's eyes were still glued to her as he stared without blinking.

Noticing the crowd outside, the Pastor paused the baptismal service. "Why is there a commotion in my churchyard?" he said.

"Satan in the churchyard trying to stop God's work, Sir," bellowed another church member.

The Pastor came closer to Genise and asked, "What is your name?" "Genise." "How old are you?".

"I'm sixteen years old."
"Where is your mother?"
Genise hesitated. "She is dead."
"Who do you live with?"
"My dad."

The Pastor then instructed one of his female members to hug Genise. For Genise, this was the first hug she had received in years. It felt protective and paused her sadness.

"Young lady, I want you to know that if you die tonight, you will go to heaven to be with the Lord," said the Pastor. "However, as much as I am not in agreement with your father's decision, I cannot baptize you. Your father is legally responsible for you until you are 18 years old, and he is unwilling to permit you to be baptized. Therefore, I must respect your father's decision." Genise's face drooped like a wilted plant.

"But –"You keep coming to church, and as soon as you celebrate your eighteenth birthday, I will baptize you," said the Pastor. He cupped Genise's face in his hands and smiled. "My child, the Lord loves you; just leave your address and the directions to your house with Sister Merle, and I will speak with your father when the time comes."

As the Pastor walked away to continue the service, Genise felt like hope walked out as well. She dragged her feet in the dirt and bit her lips as she left the churchyard. Suddenly, her school bag became a heavy load as she stared in the distance. She saw people talking, but the pain in her heart drowned their voices. Dogs howling as night fell, children screaming as they played, and the crackling fire consuming garbage – she heard none of it.

Passers-by and neighbors, some of whom attended the church, were furious. A few church leaders visited her home the same night to talk with her father and pray for him. In the days that followed, news of the incident spread like wildfire, and many people in the community accused Lester of abusing his daughter because she had no mother. Lester now had to endure a few stares that spoke louder than the insults hurled at him whenever he left his yard.

Still, he did not change his mind and warned Genise not to let the Pastor come to his house. She knew that she would never get her father's approval to join the church, so she reverted to old habits. She wore short clothes.

One day, she crossed paths with Pastor Milford. "Long time no see, young one. Which school are you attending?"

"Ardenne High School."

"Are you learning when you go to school?"

"Yes, Pastor."

"You are not learning when you come to church. Why are you so inappropriately dressed?"

"I think I am rebelling because of my father's behavior."

"You are only hurting yourself if you rebel. So, bow your head, and let us pray." The prayer brought conviction to Genise's heart. She became more conscious of her attire and knew in her heart she had acted foolishly.

She remembered having been told by one of the church members that the Pastor's daughter has the same name, 'Genise,' which could be why he was always encouraging her and praying for her. Lester's resistance wore slightly, and soon he grew to like the Pastor because he always corrected and encouraged his daughter.

Chapter 9

THE ESCAPE

Watch ye therefore, and pray always, that he may be counted worthy to escape all these things that shall come to pass, and to stand before the son of man.

~ Luke 21:36

A strong wind rattled the church windows and threatened to topple the bottle of olive oil from the rostrum. Small creatures rustled through the bushes, searching for food or trying to escape their predators. The smell of chicken foot soup invaded the nostrils of a few who could not resist the urge to satisfy their taste buds.

A small group of men, women, and children repeatedly sang the chorus:

The water is troubled, my friend.
Step right in

The water is troubled, my friend.
Step right in God Almighty power is moving every hour.

"By the confession of your faith in the Lord Jesus Christ, I now baptize you in the name of the Father, Son, and the Holy Ghost," said Pastor Milford as he immersed Genise in the pool of water. As she came up out of the pool, breaking the surface of the water, happiness rained on her. Her smile lit up the surroundings more than the high intensity bulbs that provided light to the building. The cloud of darkness that overshadowed her for so long was now lifted.

Then suddenly and unexpectedly, Norma, a friend of Genise, screamed with a loud voice saying, "Genise, you made it in! Congratulations" as she hugged her with the pearly white towel that was in her hands.

Several church members rushed to hug her after she came out of the water – their hugs felt like heaven. A few of her neighbors and her brother came to cheer for her.

Dean quickly ran to the altar and said, "Genise, I could see the bottom of your feet from the pews as soon has the Pastor immersed you in the water,

HAHA!" said Dean as he laughed gleefully.

"Here's a cup of soup; it's on me. I'm so happy for you," a neighbor said as she rubbed Genise's head. "Thank you, Miss T," Genise said with tears of joy dampening her face.

"Remember to give me your wet clothes; I wouldn't want your father to catch you." "Oh yes! thank you so much; I don't know how I can thank you enough."

She hastily changed into fresh clothing and handed the neighbor the wet ones. As she made her way to her siblings, who were waiting in the churchyard, she was enveloped with more hugs and words of encourage-ment.

"I checked, and Miss T's son is still distracting daddy," Odetta said as she embraced her sister. "It was good seeing you get baptized. It was fun to watch."

"Thanks, Detta. I can't believe I'm eighteen, and I still have to hide this from daddy."

Odetta smiled and squeezed her sister's arm. "Your secret is safe with me and Dean. I have never seen you smile like that.

I'm happy about whatever makes you happy."

The two sisters hugged each other tightly while Dean enjoyed his cup of soup.

Genise grabbed her brother. "Come here you!"

"You're welcome," Dean said as he tried to prevent his chicken foot from escaping the Styrofoam cup.

Pastor Milford chuckled. "Please allow me to interrupt; where is my hug?" He hugged Genise as she patted his back. "Are you upset that I got baptized in black clothes?" Genise asked.

"Lord, no. It is better to have a white heart and a full suit of black clothes than a black heart and a full suit of white clothes".

"Pastor, I feel brand new. I feel something that I haven't felt in forever."

"What's that?"

Genise took a deep breath and softly answered, "Peace."

"The peace of God that surpassed all understanding will guard your hearts and minds through Christ Jesus," he said. "Come inside; they are about to pray for the new converts."

This experience was a new beginning for Genise. All her life, she yearned for a family. Yes, she had a father, siblings, and grandparents, but she wanted people to understand her. She wanted a place devoid of remnants of her past. The baptism brought the healing that she needed.

Victory

"Gen, you can't stay here any longer because Miss T's son is running out of topics to continue distracting daddy," whispered Dean.

On their way home, Genise skipped and twirled with newfound joy. She picked every fruit, smelled every flower, and greeted anyone no matter how far they were. She sang bits of gospel songs that she could remember with her arms around her siblings' necks. She picked up a stick and waved it in the air as if she was directing a choir. Genise even did a short dance performance before nearing their home.

The heavy burden that she carried for so many years was now lifted off her shoulders. Genise felt unstop-pable as happiness and joy glowed inside her.

All the pains of her childhood at once faded into the distance as hope flooded her heart and mind.

As soon as Genise got into bed, the rain began to fall, the dancing pitter-patter of the raindrops on the roof was musical to her ears. The window was open, and so she could smell the sweet earthy smell as the raindrops touched the earth.

The breeze began to blow; she felt the soft wet specks across her arms as she reached for the window. She inhaled and exhaled while smiling a little as she slowly closed the windows. The rain always had a calming effect on Genise at night.

She closed her eyes; she had entered a magnificent place, moments later she gently embraced the refreshing solace of sleep.

CHAPTER 10

THE DREAM

I will instruct thee and teach thee in the way which thou shalt go, I will guide thee with my eyes.
                              ~Psalms 32:8

The next morning was beautiful. The golden rays from the sun at the start of the morning were divine.

The view of the sky from the balcony where Genise lay was breathtaking and indescribable. She could hear melodious sounds coming from nature's choirs. It was relaxing and soothing to her mind. It sounded like an orchestra:

"...*The steadfast love of the Lord never ceases,*
   His mercies never comes to an end.
   They are new every morning, new every morning. Great is thy faithfulness oh Lord, Great is thy faithfulness".

Victory

Then, she saw A GREAT BIG BOOK open, the owner of the book began to turn the pages and when he had found Genise's name in the book, he, with a rubber stamp, stamped the word SAVED across her name.

At once, Genise's heart felt also as if it was also imprinted and sealed with the words SAVED! She awoke and realized it was a dream.

"And grieve not the Holy Spirit of God, whereby ye are sealed unto the day of redemption." The words from *Ephesians 4 vs. 30 KJV* flooded Genise's heart and mind; suddenly Genise felt was an unexplainable peace.

As she lay on the bed with eyes closed, she basks in the delightful atmosphere of her new birth. She then saw what appeared to be footprints on a narrow pathway, and then Genise heard a still, small voice in the depths of her heart echoing.

"If you diligently seek after God with your whole heart, thrive after God via reading and obeying the word of God, praying, and fasting, then you will find the pathway that he has already predestined for your life. Then like a whisper, she received these instructions:

"There are two parts to the Bible: Holiness and Faith, and to be a victorious Christian, you must master both parts of the Bible. Genise, you will not struggle with holiness, but you will have to work hard on developing your faith in God".

"It is not the good that you do that impresses God. But it is your motive. God will judge men according to their motives". (The reasons for your act of kindness).

Genise got out of bed and got dressed, but suddenly realized that the inner changes she was experiencing were so profound that it also radiated on the outside and affected her very appearance.

Everywhere she went: whether walking down the street, playing with her friends or going to the local shop; many would stop her to ask what had happened to her. Genise had such joy and peace that everyone who saw her wanted to know how they could receive such joy and peace.

As the days flowed on, Genise discovered that she could do things that she could not previously do, like forgiving.

The knowledge that God had forgiven her and that he loves her felt magical. Genise knew that she had to choose whether she would pursue her dad's Rastafarian religion or her grandmother Icy witchcraft practices and rituals.

As she meditated on these things, a particular scripture resonated in her heart.

> *I call heaven and earth to record this day against you, that I have set before you; life and death, blessing and cursing: therefore, choose life that both thou and thy seed may live,* Deuteronomy 30:19.

Genise was resolute in her mind to follow and explore her newfound peace. As such, Genise never discussed her baptism with her dad because of the embarrassing church incident two years ago. His anger may have kept her away from church physically, but her heart was always there. She had entered adulthood, and she was not going to let her father steal her joy.

Thankfully, none of the neighbors divulged her secret, and they took turns calling her and reminding her to ensure that she leave church early so that she can to reach home on time. The neighbors would send message to her whenever she went to church in the evenings.

So that her dad would not lock her out of the house. She considered her neighbors and siblings as her "dream team."

After her baptism, Genise chose not to return to St. Elizabeth to visit her grandparents in the summer. Lester never forced her to visit them either. She knew that Odetta and Dean would enjoy themselves, but she wanted no part in her grandmother's strange lifestyle.

One night has she finished her devotion; Lester sat on the bed. He turned his back on her and stared out the window.

"That's your mother's family."

"My mother is dead." Genise replied

Lester got up and stood at the door. "I hope you know that you're on your own."

His words bounced off her because she had always felt alone since her mother's death.

The church was the only place that felt like home, the only place where she was truly comfortable. However, she still hid her baptism from her father. It was as if Jesus was her first boyfriend, and she had to hide the relationship. With none of her siblings at home to watch for her, she started going to church immediately after work. Unfortunately, some nights she came home very late, which did not go unnoticed by her father.

"In this life, you will never have the support of your grandparents again, so make sure you are truly serving this one true God," he said with disgust.

"I'm not going to practice their strange rituals. I don't want to offend them, so I'd rather stay away," respond-ed Genise indifferently.

"Them write you off."

"No problem."

"Icy thinks that you're proud and rude now that you have a job and getting older."

Genise laughed mockingly. "Did my dead mother tell her that?"

Lester opened his mouth, but no words came out.

"I just don't believe in all the superstition anymore," she said. "Do you know how many nightmares I have had?"

CHAPTER 11

FREEDOM

Therefore, if any man be in Christ, he is a new creature: old things are passed away. behold, all things are become new.
~**2 Corinthians 5:17**

Genise no longer thought about Icy nor the strange messages /instructions that her dead mother gave to her, no more baths with pungent vials, no more superstition or rituals.

Freedom engulfed her heart.

This was further complimented by the fact that she no longer went to St. Elizabeth to visit Icy.

Life was refreshing, though not perfect.

Genise still had challenges as Lester began to throw jabs at her faith. Lester tried to discourage Genise from practicing her newfound faith by locking her out of the house along with his repeated threats to throw both she and her belongings on the streets.

Genise would leave from work and go straight to church. Church was her happy place: It was where she felt most at ease. She could identify with the family of believers who shared similar experiences and many wonderful testimonies of how their lives had been changed by the power of God. She had also developed a very good friendship with a few of the believers they would look out for her arrival each night and would even save a seat for her beside them.

Genise's melodrama series would occur every evening as soon as she got home after church. "Nine thirty," Lester grumbled one night. He inquired of his neighbors about his daughter's whereabouts, but no one seemed to know.

Finally, by ten o'clock, Lester had no choice but to retreat to his verandah to wait for his daughter.

The stillness of the night brought about an unusual eerie feeling. He slowly sipped his ganja tea with his piercing eyes above the rim of cup every now and then, watching, waiting for Genise's return while he muttered something incoherently under his breath.

As soon as he saw Genise coming, he emptied his cup at the side of the verandah. "Miss B, so the boss asked you to work overtime tonight?"

Genise gently rubbed his arm. "Goodnight daddy, I hope your night is going well," she said.

She never understood why her father would always call her "Miss B" whenever he was upset with her. None of her names had 'B' in them.

He clenched his fists and stood at attention. "I asked you a question, Miss B," he said in a stern tone.

"Daddy, not tonight." Genise replied

"Yes! Tonight! This night! It is my house, and I need answers!"

Genise trembled. "Daddy…"

With a single mighty swing, Lester threw his cup into the bushes. "You – are – wasting my time," he said,

"You wouldn't understand," she responded

Lester moved in front of the door, blocking the entrance "I need an answer, Miss B," he said with his arms folded.

Genise's lips quivered a bit, then she swallowed hard, while tightly clutching her handbag, and confessed to her father about her baptism and going to church.

"Oh, so you turn big woman now, Miss B?" he said. "Starting tomorrow, my doors close at eight-thirty in the night because I have not sent you anywhere." Lester walked inside, slammed the door in her face and began cursing while he pushed down anything in his way. Genise slowly opened the door and went straight to bed.

"She is working in the Babylon system, and now she is also serving the white man's God. She will soon be homeless." He said to himself. He staggered into his room and entered into a boxing match with the bed. Tired and out of breath, Lester went into the closet and smelled Betty's old dress before falling on to the bed. He buried his face in her pillow that mothered his wails.

CHAPTER 12

THE INVESTMENT

Invest in seven ventures, yes, in eight. you do not know what disaster may come upon the land.
~Ecclesiastes 11:2

It was 8:45 a.m. as Genise walked briskly down the corridors of her office towards the Cashiers' section. "Genise, hurry up! Have you heard?" a voice rang out. "Heard what?" retorted Genise.

"The company is offering forty thousand (40,000) additional shares to employees who are interested because a lot of employees did not take up their share offer." The Human Resources Department has also informed us that shares can be paid for via salary deductions." Without a second thought, Genise dashed up the stairs and went straight to the Human Resources Department to put in her application. Little did Genise know that the next few seconds would change her life forever.

To exercise her right to take up the additional shares in the company Genise, hurriedly made her way from her workstation and head upstairs to The Human Resource Department. Upstairs she met her friend.

Michael a member of the department and asked him for the share option and salary deduction form. Michael, without hesitation, gave her the form, she filled it out; he signed it and processed her on his system. After which she left hurriedly as she made her way to her workstation, before her supervisor had the chance to notice her disappearance from the Cashiers/Tellers' section. There were already many customers in the queue waiting to be served.

Later, that morning the company sent an email to all staff informing them that they had closed the share offer.

At noon, it was announced that the share prices had *"jumped"* from two dollars ($2.00) to fourteen dollars ($14.00) per share.

Genise could not contain her excitement, so she rushed to the powder room, where she called her friend and gave her the good news. The events of today had brought unexpected joy and she could hardly maintain her composure as she attended to the customers.

The weeks went by quickly; Genise sold her shares and made a deposit on a House! To her surprise, the mortgage company said that her salary was one and a half million ($1.5 m) below the threshold for her to qualify for a mortgage. Genise was devastated.

At lunch, she shared her disappointment with a colleague, who offered to offer her support and joint her salary with hers so that she could secure a joint mortgage arrangement so that she could qualify to get the house.

This, however, had implications for any future sale of the property as the friend's name would have to be included in the title as joint owner. The mortgage officer further explained the nuisances of her decision and that any changes to the ownership of the property title would require legal proceedings through the courts and that it would be very costly for example if she in the future opted to remove her friend's name from her title. The lawyer informed her that the legal fee for doing so would normally be a percentage of the current market value of the property.

Genise was unfazed by this explanation and was instead resolute in her mind that nothing would prevent her from making her investment in the newly built property; so, with that the mortgage officer accepted her application.

The morning was quiet. Too quiet! The birds had fallen silent and even the wind seemed to have died down. Everything was as still, and as dead and dark as the grave.

At midday, Genise was told by her supervisor to report to the mortgage unit. The manager had left an envelope for her and had to leave for an urgent meeting. Genise at once took the envelope, went to the lady's room, locked the door and opened the envelope. She discovers a mortgage commitment letter. Reading the letter, she also noticed that the monthly mortgage payments for the property were three quarters of her monthly salary. Despite the high monthly payments, Genise was jubilant! She fell on her knees and gave God all the praise!

On her way home that evening she received a call from the manager in the mortgage department who informed Genise that The Mortgage Committee had given her a message to convey to Genise, which says: "You are your own worst enemy, it was very silly of you to joint with your friend/co-worker to qualify for a mortgage, your decision literally means that your co-worker will be a part of your life for the rest of your life, and when she dies, her children will pursue you. As such we the members of the Mortgage Committee have unanimously decided to help you by *"taking the rope from around your neck"* and have decided to give you the mortgage, even though you do not earn enough to qualify for the mortgage. Therefore, they have asked me to tell you that you should rent out one of the rooms in the house so that you will be able to afford the monthly mortgage payments. The committee also said that they admire you because you are a very ambitious young woman!" The mortgage manager concluded by also offering her own congratulations to Genise on becoming a homeowner and told her to report to the mortgage unit and sign the mortgage deed and documents in the morning and to bring them to the housing developers!

As such in the fullness of time, her accommodation problems were resolved. At last, when she bought her first home at 25 years old. She packed her belongings in boxes and cleaned the room before leaving. The mysterious and unexpected letter she received did not evoke any emotion in Genise. Instead, she decided to tear up the letter in pieces.

Later that evening while driving on route to her new house Genise opened her hands, sending the torn pieces of the letter flying behind.

Her dad and grandparents were all shocked. And the most beautiful thing was that the Lord also caused Lester to construct all the inner grills for the inside windows and doors in her house - and the outer gate that surrounded her house to secure her and her property since he was an astute electrical welder.

CHAPTER 13

NEW BEGINNING

Behold, I will do a new thing, now it shall spring forth, shall you not know it? I will even make a road in the wilderness and rivers in the desert.
                              ~Isaiah 43:19

Genise turned and looked into her abandoned room for the last time. The place she once despised, but had painfully learnt to endure.

A flood of emotions filled her heart, as she reflected on the many episodes of her young life. She had many memories of her upbringing. Beautiful ones, sad ones, memories of unexpressed feelings and untold sacrifices, and in that moment Genise exhaled and smiled softly. She now felt as if a new life was breathed into her.

As she went out of the room, she waved goodbye to Lester. This was her moment of triumph. She was about to step into a new chapter of her life.

"Genise, where are you going?" boomed Lester. Genise paused, looked up and dangled her keys close to his face. "To my new home, I have bought a house!" She replied with a pleasing smile on her face.

Lester laughed out loud. "Liar," he responded

"The moving man is coming in a few minutes, so if you could be so kind as to help me put my things in the van when it gets here, I'd be grateful."

To Lester's surprise, the moving van arrived within a few minutes. As Genise began to move out her belongings, he stood there riveted to the spot of ground unable to come to terms with what was transpiring right before him.

Lester never moved a hand to assist Genise with taking her belongings to the van. It was as if his hands had become paralyzed.

With his face void of emotions, he saw his daughter doing what he never thought she was capable of with all her belongings now packed and ready to go, she turned to her dad to bid him her final goodbye.

"Good to see you young folks moving up," said the driver with a smile as they left the precinct of what used to be her former home.

Genise gave him a faint smile before reflecting on the contents of the mysterious and unexpected letter Icy had sent her. YOU HAVE NEGLECTED ALL LOVE AND CARE I GAVE YOU. Therefore, WHEN I DIE, DO NOT COME TO MY FUNERAL. IF YOU DO, I WILL SLAP YOU IN YOUR FACE.," it had read.

The letter still did not evoke any emotion in Genise. Instead, according to her earlier plan she tore the letter to pieces, cupped them in her hands and sent them flying outside the window of the van.

The van came to a stop as they finally reached their destination. This was a new day and new life wherein lieth new opportunities for her.

Getting out of the van, Genise embraced the warmth of the sunshine. Knowing that this was a new day and new life filled with endless possibilities. She could now "spread her wings" and soar as high as she wanted in this her newfound freedom.

Her faith told her that it was never too late to start over.

As evening came and the sky became covered with darkness a full moon arose in its splendor illuminating the dark night sky. It was her first night in her magnificent new home, a new beginning and it was beautiful.

Genise found comfort under her cozy blanket and as she prayed tears clouded her eyes, a single drop rolled down her cheeks.

She remembered her childhood and could not believe that she had survived all that pain. She never dreamed that she would own her own home at 25 years old. She lifted her hands thanking God for how He had blessed her and for all the things He has made possible in her life: she was in a new community, in a new house, she was a newly installed member of her church youth chorale, where she travelled across the island and ministered the good news in songs. Everything in her life was perfect and refreshing. So, with a heart full of joy Genise laid her head on her comfortable pillow she drifted into dreamland.

CHAPTER 14

MISSIONS

How beautiful on the mountains, are the feet of him who brings good news, who proclaims peace, who brings glad tidings of good things, who proclaim salvation. who says to Zion, "Your God reigns!"
~Isaiah 52:7

Genise never had one dull day in her newfound life as a Christian. When it was not her father, it was the people at her workplace. Thinking about it still brings a smile to her face. Her colleagues would tease her about not having a boyfriend.

They asked her all types of questions about how she managed without a boyfriend. They also wanted to know how she coped with not having a sexual relationship, and they would spend a lot of time telling her about all that she was missing. They would always tease her and tell her that she was too holy, righteous, and foolish. Some people in her community and at work even nicknamed her "*Welder's Virgin Mary.*" Once again, she became one of the most talked-about people at work. However, that did not bother her, because she was also one of the most successful people in her community and workplace. As a member of the youth chorale, she traveled with the team and performed in all fourteen (14) parishes of Jamaica. They also traveled to the Cayman Islands on mission.

Genise not only ministered in singing, but she also prayed for, encouraged, and evangelized in the communities nearby wherever they ministered. There were approximately forty people on the youth chorale; this allowed the members of the Chorale to put on crusades, street, and tent meetings. There were also ministers on the chorale, and an Evangelist was also assigned to travel with the team. Her days were serving and traveling to rallies, going to retreats, putting on productions and street meetings around the island were some of her best years as a young, zealous Christian. She also served as assistant Sunday School Treasurer, Sunday School Teacher, and Alter worker.

She also worked closely with a Missionary who worked to help the indigent. She would aid her to cook and distribute food to people living on the street. Genise spent a lot of her time volunteering and helping her in ministry. She wrote sponsorship letters and sent them to various companies. Assist her with her bible school assignments, wrote the messages that she would preach on her numerous preaching engagements, assist her to book her flights and anything else that she needed assistance in achieving for her ministry.

At one point, she even went and lived with her for a brief period. She kept herself very busy with church-related activities in those early years. Genise loved being a Christian.

Victory

Up to that time, she never experienced anything she could not overcome. However, that was about to change very soon.

CHAPTER 15

The Betrayal

If was an enemy who mocked me, I could endure it, if it was an opponent boasting over me, I could hide myself from him. But it was you my companion, my colleague and close friend. We had intimate talks together and walked together in the temple.
~ Psalm 55:12-14

The piercing ring of the telephone shrilled through the peaceful night, jolting Genise who had her head down doing practice questions for her exam. Genise abruptly stopped as her eyes roamed the room for her mobile phone. The loud ring of the phone directed her attention to the couch nearby. Genise picked up the phone and answered.

"Hello."

"Hello, Genise, this is sister Donna." Pleasantly, surprised, she realized it was her good friend Donna from church. She began to tell Genise that she had been trying to locate her to ask her for a small favor, Donna explained that she had been

Victory

evicted from her apartment and had nowhere to go. She asked Genise if she could temporarily accommodate her for a few months until she found an apartment of her own. She further explained that she had been trying unsuccessfully to find suitable accommodation. Genise was happy to hear from her good friend Donna and without any thought offered to assist Donna.

Unknown to Genise that this act of kindness that she extended to Donna would change her life forever! The months moved quickly by, and Genise had grown to enjoy the comradery and eventful weekends with Donna and some of the members of her church. Donna had a lot of friends who quickly also became friends with Genise because of her act of Christ-like kindness that she showed Donna.

One Saturday morning Genise, now a budding accountant, packed her books and placed them quickly into her handbag as she dashed towards the door on route to the library to study, the library opening hours were from 9:00 a.m. to 2 p.m. on Saturdays.

Donna noticed that Genise was leaving and stopped her briefly and invited her to a prayer meeting that would be held at her friend's house who was also a member of their church. Genise was unable to confirm her attendance at the prayer meeting in the moment but promised Donna that if she felt strong enough after studying at the library she would attend.

Genise left the library promptly at 2pm. Feeling energized and fulfilled, Genise decided that she would retreat to the prayer meeting to celebrate and refresh her mind and spirit. A few minutes later, Genise got a taxi and headed to the prayer meeting. The afternoon breeze was cool and refreshing.

Genise's mind drifted to a few days earlier and remembered that Frank, an eligible bachelor from her church, a recent bible school graduate and a minister in her church approached her for a date, he also told Genise that he was attracted to her and was interested in pursuing a close friendship with her.

Genise, though fond of Minister Frank, was unsure whether she wanted to pursue a long-term friendship with him, a feeling of uncertainty clouded Genise's mind. The thoughts swirl around in Genise's head. Was it a good idea to go on a date with Frank? She did not want to send him the wrong signal.

Genise thoughts were interrupted by the sudden honking of the horn, from the taxi driver's attempt to get the attention of one of his friends he saw along the roadway. The traffic flowed freely, soon Genise was off the taxi and started the five-minutes' walk towards the house on route to the prayer meeting. Upon arrival at the house, she could hear the voices of the children as they shrieked with joy playing in the yard. The house was in a residential community and had a big yard and a veranda. Genise proceeded to open the outer gate.

What transpired next was so heart wrenching, it plunged Genise into unimaginable pain that would impact her Christianity, faith in God, and scarred her for several years to come. Soon Genise discovered that her close friend Donna had broken her trust out of jealousy, knowing that Frank, who was one of her close friends and was also a part of their prayer group had shown interest in pursuing a friendship with Genise.

This displeased the members of the prayer group, they thought that Genise was not a right fit for Frank. So, in a desperate attempt Donna colluded with her friends to attack Genise's character. They were aware of Frank's growing interest in Genise, so they skillfully crafted a plot to tarnish her reputation, integrity, self-esteem and self-worth. Garth a bible school graduate and one of Frank's close friends like Donna and the rest of the prayer group, felt that Frank should instead date Tracey a member of the Youth Chorale who was also one of his close friends, so he too proceeded with their plot.

Upon entering the yard, Noelene came to the door and opened the locks to the house. Garth, who was tall, dark and handsome was a budding minister at the church an intercessor, beckoned to Genise to come in and he indicated that he was going to pray for her.

The prayer group consisted of Noelene, Donna and Fay who were all praise & worship leaders, the additional members of the group were, Winnie who was a senior member of the church and Pam who was a former member of the church and was visiting from overseas. The members present age group ranged from mid-thirties to early forties. Genise, was the youngest, a member of the Youth Chorale was zealous and felt impressed to be included in their prayer group.

Soon Genise found herself in the middle of a circle as all six members that were present surrounded her.

Garth began to make loud utterances and to suggest that Genise was in a sexual relationship and was living a deceptive life, one filled with fornication and sin. Thus, he began to pray for Genise and placed his right hand on Genise's head, and with a loud voice spoke!

"Genise, God said to tell you that you are boastful, not living right, and you walk with a pomp, but God says he is going to cut you down! He then continued in a loud, stern voice and said.... "Genise, do you remember, Miriam, Moses's sister in the bible who, had a problem with Moses, because he married an Ethiopian woman?" and God "punished her and cut her down and made an example out of her: she became leprous like snow; this God did because of his servant Moses who she had despised because he married an Ethiopian woman!, Genise, be warned a thing is about to happen and when you hear about it, you will drop dead like Miriam!", the other members of the prayer group also began to agree with Garth shouting the name of Jesus!

Genise was shocked and speechless as she tried in that moment to process what was happening, and to understand what on earth Garth was talking about! Genise could feel the blood rushing to her head, she was confused, and felt as if she was being viciously attacked, stepping backwards away from Garth, she removed his right hand from off her head and moved out of their circle as she whispered Je--sus, Je--sus.

Suddenly she felt the Spirit of the Lord, who came abruptly upon her, and in a loud voice and with authority, Genise said, "Examine your own selves, before me, said God! examine your own selves before me said God! as she pointed to each member and sternly prophesied.

Immediately, a sudden silence struck the room, her prophetic utterances pierced the atmosphere, and for a few minutes nobody moved, even the children were frozen. A few minutes later, the phone rang - the silence was broken. Winnie, the owner of the house, went to answer the phone in the other room. Noelene, then started to verbally attack Genise, looking down at her and in a condescending manner barked...

"It's not biblical for you to prophesy!'.

Suddenly, the other six members of the group joined and started shouting at Genise the blood of Jesus! the blood of Jesus, is against you!

Garth then with a loud voice then addressed the meeting and said "Genise, God told me, that the devil was going to send you has an agent to mash-up our prayer meeting", and with that he shouted with a loud voice has he pointed his finger towards the door and in a supercilious manner said "LEAVE!", "LEAVE!"

But Genise, couldn't feel her feet, she was transfixed to the floor. Garth became enraged.

"GET OUT! GET OUT! And you cannot put Donna out of your house!

The other members of the group including Donna began to plea the blood of Jesus! the blood of Jesus"! Genise lifted her hands in the air and said, "okay, I will leave'.

Winnie, the owner of the house, escorted Genise to the door, but she could not find the keys to let Genise out of the house! They all began to desperately search for the keys to open the gate.

Finally, the keys were found, a few minutes later and Genise left.

What was Garth talking about? Had God really given him a message for me? The thoughts raced through Genise's mind, as the tears welled up in her eyes, she could feel a piercing pain deep within her heart, she felt demonized and betrayed by the attacks that were meted out to her by the members of the prayer group and church brethren who were also members of her church *(especially Donna who was her close friend, my sister, who betrayed me while at the same time living under my roof!).*

By the time Genise finally got home she was overwhelmed, exhausted and in continuous tears at the day's event.

At 7p.m. that evening Donna came through the door and attempted to give her a box of Jerk Chicken that she had brought, Genise just stood there weak and motionless as the recent events replayed in her mind. She did not utter a single word; her mind was bombarded. Millions of thoughts rushed through her mind, she was confused and felt a sudden pounding headache. To calm down she immediately left the room where Donna was and went straight to bed, where she cried and after an hour, she gradually calmed down and slowly drifted off to sleep that night.

CHAPTER 16

The Meltdown

"I had fainted, unless I had believed to see the goodness of the Lord in the land of the living.
Wait on the LORD: be of good courage, and he shall strengthen thine heart: wait, I say, on the LORD".
~ Psalm 27:13-14

The betrayal from the revered prayer group and from Donna, spiraled Genise in a series of emotional and spiritual turmoil. Genise felt that she could no longer trust Donna. So, the next morning after breakfast despite the awkwardnesses of the previous evening's event, Genise had a meeting with Donna, asking her to leave and giving her one month's notice to move out of her house.

Donna agreed to leave and apologized to Genise on behalf of the prayer group. Genise then left for church, while Donna stayed home. By the time Genise arrived at church it was just in time for praise and worship and to Genise surprised Garth was leading the praise and worship along with Novelene.

At the sight of Garth Genise could feel her heart skipped a beat, she was furious, why didn't God strike him dead, since he a devil on Saturday and Christian on Sunday! Genise tried to fight off the myriads of thoughts that flooded her mind. A sudden feeling of sadness and despair came upon Genise.

Garth could be seen dancing as he led the congregation into worship. Novelene also seems to be enjoying worship too. Genise, however, could not concentrate on worship, she tried closing her eyes to focus on worship, but this proved futile.

Yesterday's memory of Garth, Novelene and the rest of the prayer group's pronouncements and, agreement, Garth said that "God said that he's going to cut you down, and you will drop dead, because of pride", replayed in Genise's mind. The impact of the hatred that was meted to her made her unable to bear the pain that crushed her heart and caused great difficulties for her to worship God. So, Genise took up her handbag and Bible and left for her home.

By the time she arrived home she observed that Donna had already moved out. Genise, broken-hearted, went and lay down on the bed and started sobbing, she had no appetite for food, she just wanted to lie in the dark and cry.

The next few days, after Donna left, Genise spiraled further into depression, losing interest in attending church or speaking to any member of her church. So, she changed all her cell numbers, as she now sees Garth, Donna and Novelene as deceptive and two-faced and wanted nothing more to do with them.

The weeks progressed and Genise gradually lost interest in reading her bible or attending church. She found herself unable to pray and was angered that God did not punish the prayer group for what they had done to her. She also observed that all the members of the prayer group's life went on as usual. But Genise felt stuck and unable to move on as she had no support system carrying the hurt and pain alone, she decided not to report the prayer group to the Pastor of the church or any of the members of her church, so she kept the matter to herself.

Whenever Genise took lunch break from work she would go to the powder room or ladies' room and cry. She had a lingering headache; it was as if she had a crown of pain around her head. She suffered from insomnia, loss of memory, dizziness and tremors; Genise could not even hold her teacup in one hand without support from the other hand.

The rapid decline in Genise health were so overwhelming that she sought help from an Intercessor, who invited Genise home, prayed for her and did her best to encourage her. The Intercessor encouraged Genise to play the audio bible at nights and gave her a few gospel CDs.

Genise tried to find solace in the worship CD's and for a season they worked. But after a while even the gospel CDs became repulsive to her; soon she did not want to listen to any gospel music or any form of religious programs.

One day Genise was invited to a prophetic meeting by one of her co-workers, she decided to attend since she dreaded the thought of being home alone on a Friday evening. Upon arrival at the meeting Genise went and sat at the back of the church and just sat in the service, she didn't have the energy to participate in service and was unable to concentrate. After almost an hour, Genise lost interest in the service, so she picked up her handbag and moved quickly towards the direction of the door. Suddenly, she was stopped by a hand that held on to her shoulder, looking around she saw that it was one of the prophets, he placed his arms around her and directed her to the altar at the front of the church.

The prophet then asks Genise her name and tells her that the Lord loves her and has seen her tears and will deliver her from all her pain and restore her strength. Genise just stood there, she felt no emotions, it was as if his words went from one ear to the next. The prophet asks the congregation to stretch their hands towards her and two of the other prophets join by laying their hands on her shoulder and along with the members of the church begin to earnestly pray for Genise.

As they prayed and prophesied that she would live and not die. Genise, tried to fight off the tears, but the tears flowed down her cheeks. After they had finished praying, Genise quietly left the service and walked briskly towards the bus stop. The journey home was soothing, the breeze was cold, and she could feel the tension loosening from around her heart as peace slowly flooded her heart and mind. Genise arrived home and no longer had tears in her eyes, the prayer work and provided her with the comfort she needed to fall asleep that evening reflecting on the words of the prophet. Genise finally felt that she was healed and had the strength to return to church and chorale practice.

That night Genise had no idea that her peace would be short-lived and that she would need to be resolute in her mind to keep her joy over the next few days.

CHAPTER 17

Un-forgiveness

But I say unto you which hear, love your enemies, do good to them which hate you, bless them that curse you, and pray for them which despitefully use you.
~Luke 6:27-28

Genise wrestled with God in her heart and mind as she struggled with un-forgiveness. She had an overwhelming awareness that God was urging her to forgive the members of the prayer group, as forgiving others was his command. But Genise wanted the members of the prayer group to feel the pain that they had put her through. Genise consistently blocked out the overwhelming thoughts of the need to forgive that stirred deep within her heart. God seemingly didn't care, but demanded that she forgive them! But Genise disagreed, because she was the one who was wronged and had suffered great injustices at the hands of the evil prayer group.

Genise even started to get very angry with God. And blatantly started to argue with God within her heart. She consistently disobeyed and ignored the prompting and command of the Holy Spirit to forgive the members of the prayer group that had caused her great hurt.

A series of questions flooded Genise's mind. Questions of whether God was real or even existed. If God is real, why didn't he punished or strike them? Daily, Genise pondered these thoughts in her heart.

Her inner voice was telling her that God had let her down and telling her that if her God could sit back and let a prayer group treat her so badly, then it makes no sense she served that God anymore.

Genise continued to question God's existence as she spiraled downwards; First, she had suffered the trauma of experiencing the loss of her mother mysteriously at the age of six, secondly, she had no one talk to, not even a single person support system. Her father was angry with her for getting baptized and came to the church and publicly humiliated her. She now felt too embarrassed to tell her father how the members of the prayer group had treated her. Because her father, an ardent Rastafarian, had consistently warned her not to mix-up with or have anything to do with the Babylon church people them and to stop worship the white Jesus.

Genise was heartbroken and felt let down by the church, being a young girl, she had to navigate and endure the myriads of challenges single-handedly. Now she had to deal with this evil prayer group, who had invoked the curse of death upon her using the name and blood of Jesus.

The members of the prayer group were all older than her and had their families and their support system to go home to; as ministers of the church, they knew better, yet instead of guiding, protecting and encouraging Genise's faith as a

Victory

new convert, they colluded to cause her ultimate demise, they showed no remorse.

Genise felt as if her whole world had collapsed and there was nothing, she could have done to prevent it from happening. She felt helpless, lost and felt as if she was slowly losing her mind. There was a dense feeling of confusion in her heart and mind that caused her to constantly drift in and out of depression. It was as if a tape recorder of all these events constantly replayed in her head, and she could not get it to stop.

Genise believed that the prayer group was a disgrace to the church and to the body of Christ and had seemingly proved her father right. She now knew that the members of the prayer group were evil, and this made it very difficult for her to forgive them. At times the unresolved and painful memories would trigger headaches. It felt like an impenetrable black cloud had covered her heart and mind and felt as if her entire being was slowly shutting down. She was on the brink of back-sliding. These intense feelings and thoughts continued during the night as she wrestled.

The next morning Genise eyes popped open while she was still in bed with a hardened heart, still unwilling to forgive her friends, when suddenly her heart began to beat very fast, and without warning she felt as if someone had leaned over and turned off a switch inside her.

Later, that day she realized that each time she took up the newspaper or any form of literature to read, her head felt like it was about to explode. She also realized that she was unable to recognize people whom she knew or was familiar with.

That Sunday morning, upon her arrival at church, she saw one of her church brothers who was her friend standing by the door. Genise attempt to greet him so she called him by his name and said," hello Michael", has she walked by, but to

Genise surprise he turned around and in a stern tone he answered, "Genise, my name is not Michael, my name is ONEIL", He further said, "Genise be careful, that you are not slipping up on God!", as he walked away angrily. She felt as if she had lost fifty percent of her brain functionality, Genise just stood there in bewilderment, she scrambled towards her seat, trying to compose herself.

It was as if God was still reprimanding her, because the message the preacher preached that morning to the congregation, was that every time an individual disobeyed God, it is likened to the wax from a lit candle that falls on that person's heart and overtime, if that person continues to disobey God, the wax will become so hard, until that person's heart becomes a stone and then die within them!

As Genise listened to the message she realized that she was in trouble with God based on what she heard. At the end of the message, the church service was dismissed. Suddenly, Genise started to realize that all the people she saw in church all had familiar and pleasant faces, but she did not know their names or recognize them. Whenever anybody greeted her, she would smile and hurriedly walk away, to avoid conversing with them. She couldn't risk anyone knowing that she was going senile. The journey home from church that day was a long one as Genise pondered the day's experience deep within her heart.

CHAPTER 18

The Encounter

And he said, hear now my words: If there be a prophet among you, I the LORD will make myself known unto him in a vision, and will speak un to him in a dream.
~Numbers 12:6-8

Loss of appetite, heart palpitations, insomnia, restlessness, and tremors plagued Genise over the next few days. She even began to question her Christianity and whether God even loved her.

"Why did I feel so heart-broken? Why was I feeling so lost? Where is God in all of this? Is it because, I am in the early stage of my Christian life and I had secretly fell in love with Frank? was it because Garth and the prayer group had laughed at me because Frank got married, and are now they are publicly laughing and gloating, every time, I see them at church or within the community?". These questions raged in

Genise's heart and mind and consistently prevented her from forgiving the members of the prayer group. Life no longer made sense to her; she felt as if she had nothing to live for anymore.

At times she would go across the road without even looking right or left, since it didn't matter to her whether she lived or died. One fateful evening as she was crossing a busy road, as she approached the middle of the road, she decided in her mind that it was useless to go across to the other side.

To Genise surprise she could not move her feet, they were glued to the street, the cars raced towards her at the T-Junction where she was crossing; suddenly the stop light turned red, and the cars slowed-down and stopped at her feet. It took all the strength in Genise's body to cross over to the other side of the road, as soon as she had finished crossing the road she just sat on the sidewalk in complete shock trying to process what had just happened.

She felt as if she had had enough and was overwhelmed with insurmountable problems that she was experiencing one after the other with no solution or justice from God in sight.

Life just didn't make sense anymore. The downward spiral continued. Soon Genise started feeling as if she was going to die. The day drifted swiftly and soon it was Sunday. The Communion Service was well attended; however, Genise managed to sit at the back of the church. As the choir sang about Jesus's love, Genise felt like a hypocrite; she no longer felt like Jesus loved her, so she consciously made the decision to just sit, watch the service and not participate in the corporate worship session. The frustration welled up in her heart as she became increasingly fed up with life and all the problems that she faced. She desired to try a different way of living to see what else is out in the world that she could try, explore or experiment. It had to be more fun than her current experiences in church.

When Genise left church that evening, she had no idea that the supernatural vision and encounter that was in store for her would rock her entire world; causing a paradigm shift that raised her awareness, showing her what was important in life. That supernatural encounter propelled her into a new dimension with the Lord, and would successfully refresh and restore her soul, empowering her with the abundant blessings she needed to fulfil her destiny.

Upon her arrival home she opened the door and stepped inside, and with a loud voice she said … "Lord I am done with church and all the crosses people in the church, I want to find a man that drives a BMW motor vehicle who can take me out and show me a goodtime". "Lord, even having babies must be better than this, I am tired! I give -up".

Instantly as the words left Genise's mouth, she was taken in an open vision, it was as if she entered a trance: suddenly she was in a boxing ring, her opponent punched her under her chin and she fell backwards to the floor both her hands and her legs spread wide apart, she felt as if she was slipping out of consciousness. Then like a whimper against the silence, she heard a distinct voice calling her Genise". She looked up, the doors were shut. A handsome man in a white robe and sandals, just appeared in front of her, she knew it was JESUS!

In that moment her mind could not process what her eyes saw, "she vividly remembered thinking, MY God, My God, I can't believe that I have allowed the church people to cause me to lose my mind…OH MY GOD, she exclaimed, I have lost my Mind! She tried to talk herself out of the experience, she whispered, this is not real, this can't be happening. Her thoughts where abruptly interrupted, when Jesus stood at her torso, and like a referee in a boxing ring ready to call the knock-out and pronounced the game over.

Jesus said, "Genise have you given up?".

She replied, "Yes Lord, I give-up, I am done!" Jesus said.... "Nine", *like a referee in a boxing ring counting down to pronounce the knock-out!*.

He again asked... "Genise have you given up?". She again replied ... "Yes, Lord, this is it!"

Jesus continued the count down, being "Eight", based on her response he continued to count down... "Three" Suddenly, Genise saw another vision.

This time, she saw a projector, and, on the screen, she saw a vision of herself in St. Elizabeth with her cousin Sally. A dog had died and laid on its back with its four feet in the air, Genise and Sally took up the dead dog; she held two of the dog's feet while Sally held the other two feet, they carried it to a corner of the bush. Where they then got an old car tyre, gasoline and a match and lit a fire and set the dead dog ablaze.

Immediately after, the screen disappeared. Then Genise saw two shadows enter the room and began to slowly lift her from the floor, one of the shadows began to lift her two hands and the other her two feet. (The same way she and her cousin Sally lifted the dead dog and carried it away to be burnt).

Then immediately, she vividly had an acute awareness that just like the dead dog, she will be taken to be burnt knowing what was happening, in a whisper, she tried to talk herself out of the experience, she softly whispered to herself; this is not real. This can't be happening. But her thoughts were abruptly interrupted when Jesus started to speak again.

Jesus again asked the question... "Genise have you given up?" Realizing the seriousness of the situation that she was experiencing.

She responded..." Lord, one last time".

Victory

And with that Jesus left the room and the two shadows followed behind him., she had no strength left, she just laid there motionless and in awe.

Genise woke up to the feeling of the tough floor on the ceramic tiles on which she laid, she could hear the voices of her neighbors and their children as they went about their morning activities.

Genise still awe stricken, laid there most of the morning still trying to process what had happened!

CHAPTER 19

London

I have been young, and now am old; yet have I not seen the righteous forsaken, nor his seed begging bread.

*~***Psalms 37:25**

The next few months sped quickly by, and an unexpected new chapter had open in Genise's life; an opportunity had arisen for her to travel to London, United Kingdom (UK) to study. Genise was excited as the opportunity represented a new beginning for her, a brand-new start, the chance to make new friends and to pursue further studies. Genise's aunt Marie agreed to support her financially during her studies in the UK.

Marie, Genise's aunt (Lester's Sister) came to Jamaica and congratulated her on her success in getting acceptance into College in the UK. During Marie's visit to the island, they got to spend quality time together. Marie told Genise how successful she was in the UK, and said that she had her own house, car and that all her three children were now adults and reside with their own husbands and families. She explained that she lived with her fiancée and had plenty of space to accommodate her during studies in the UK.

It took a few months for Genise to finalize her plans before her departure from Jamaica to the UK. Genise had to get mittens, scarves and coat for her trip as she made the transition to the UK. She knew that as an international student, there would be challenges to overcome, but she was hopeful and ready to face them.

Upon Genise's arrival in the UK, her Aunt Marie received her at the Airport. Genise enjoyed the journey to her aunt's home, she saw the double-decker buses, and the beautiful brick buildings.

As soon as they arrived at her aunt's house. Her aunt helped her with her suitcase and carried her upstairs to her room and left to go to the kitchen. Genise entered the room and was shocked by its measly furnishing, it was completely opposite to her aunt's description. The room was narrow, a small bunk bed was pushed up against the wall, there was no mattress. One half of the bed had three settee cushions and old clothes were spread out to make up the other half of the bed. The bed was tiny and short lengthwise. There was no chest of drawers for her to put her clothes in or any mirror for her to use. Genise was so frightened by what she had seen, she just stood there in disbelief, never had she imagined seeing this level of poverty in LONDON!

"Oh God, what have I gotten myself into", she thought in distress. The thoughts swirled around in Genise's mind, to think that Marie, came to Jamaica and boasted about her great success in the UK. Now to come to the UK and see that she lives below the poverty line. She didn't even have a mattress to sleep on. Marie never thought Genise would ever visit the UK to uncover the truth.

Suddenly, Genise thoughts were interrupted when she heard her name. "Genise, Genise" she could hear Marie calling her downstairs. Genise scrambled down the stairs as she tried to maintain her composure.

Marie then began to speak and said... "Genise, this is the house address, I don't expect you to leave the house, unless I give you permission". "You are not permitted to use the house phone; I will need the name and number of all the friends or anyone else that you meet at college".

"Who is Marie speaking to?", Genise questioned in her mind... she got so angry she replied... "Marie, I believed I had made a mistake in coming to London, can I borrow your land line, so that I can call the airline and book my return flight home to Jamaica?"

This made Marie furious, and she shouted... "You have embarrassed me, what will people think if you arrived in London and leave the next day?!".

A loud commotion was then heard; the sound of the door banging, Marie was interrupted. A fight had broken out, her two daughters were swearing, shouting. and fighting, the altercation involved a knife, her eldest daughter had stolen a blouse from the store a few days prior and her sister had worn it. She picked up a knife and threatened her sister, they were swearing and shouting and chasing each other around the house.

Marie, then shouted...

"Genise, don't just stand there! help me hold Anna so that I can take the knife away from her". Anna was much taller than Genise who tried to hold on to her, but Anna just pushed Genise out of her way violently and left that evening and never returned. So, Marie gave Genise Anna's room that had a bed, instead of allowing her to sleep on her old clothes and the three-settee cushion that night.

Genise's laid on the bed and was uncomfortable, her feet hung over the single bed and the room was very cold, there was no heating in the room, her aunt had not re-charged her gas card to gain access to heating. Genise just lay there trying to process her eventful day, heartbroken, as the tears fell from her eyes. To think that Marie tried to place restrictions on her, when she couldn't even control her teenage daughters, was unbelievable.

The next morning, Marie was so embarrassed with her daughters' behavior, she lifted all the restrictions she had placed on Genise. She confessed to Genise that she had no tube/train fare to take her to register for college. And told her that she needed her assistance to purchase groceries, because she had no income and solely relied on the fifty pounds she receives in benefits from the government, and that for her to qualify for it she had to do three days' community service work.

Genise felt hurt and distress, Marie had deliberately deceived her, when she boasted about how successful she was in London and about the car she owned. In reality Marie lived below the poverty line. She and her teenage daughters lived in a government council flat, she could not even maintain the electric charge card to provide heating for the house and at times she was even out of food. Genise was so deeply saddened it even affected her studies. Having to take on the additional burden of buying household groceries and paying for her aunt's household expenses was distressing.

One evening Genise went home from college, opened the door only to find out that Marie had thrown out her suitcase and books and removed the bed from the room where she slept. And left a message for Genise with her fiancée, asking her to leave her house, because she was no longer welcome there.

Genise felt betrayed and used by her aunt, for as soon as Genise was out of money, her aunt kicked her out of her house. Genise, then left the house and has she walked towards the high street she called her friend Bev, a Jamaican, a Customer Service Representative that she had met at the tube/train station on her way from college one evening and they became friends.

Bev answered the phone and Genise told Bev all that her aunt had done to her. And like an angel, Bev came to Genise's rescue. Bev offered her a job three days per week to babysit her small children in exchange for lodging. She also helped Genise to get a part-time job at McDonald's Fast-Food Restaurant to further take care of her other out of pocket expenses. Genise had to make the decision to humble herself and work at McDonald's to make ends meet, but she was very grateful to God and choose not to despise the small beginnings that God had miraculously provided for her. Instead Genise remained focused and navigated her way through to the completion of her course in the UK. Genise was awarded a University accreditation and returned home to Jamaica.

CHAPTER 20

Victory

For the Lord your God is the one who goes with you to fight for you against your enemies to give you victory.
~**Deuteronomy 20:4**

Genise watching the beautiful sunset by her window; her gazed shifted to her recently framed Professional Certified Coach Certificate, (PCC) a feeling of accomplishment washed over her. She is now a trained and certified coach equipped to guide people through their life's journey to self-development and personal growth.

A poor little girl from a very challenging background had to overcome overwhelming odds.

Genise now enjoys financial stability, with a resolute mindset and her relentless determination to seek God's forgiveness she had finally broken-free from the curses that held members of her family captive.

Genise also attained university accreditation and Accounting and Auditing Certifications and currently holds one of the top offices in government. And in an unexpected twist of events, years later Genise *"married"*, Frank!

****

As Genise reflects on the patterns that plagued her maternal side of family: all her aunts all died before they reached age of forty years old, her mom only lived to the age twenty -four years old. Genise's mother and her aunts all died young leaving behind children ages two to six years' old.

The generational curse of untimely deaths that caused an aura of sadness on her maternal side of family had not prevailed against her. Through Christ she had miraculously prevail and now looks forward with renewed hope and happiness as she continues to embark on her journey to a life of complete victory as written in Deuteronomy 30:19 which states:

> *I call heaven and earth to record this day against you, that I have set before you, life and death, blessing and cursing: therefore, choose life that both thou and thy seed may live.*

The End.

About the Author

Denise, a Jamaican- native is a very pleasant and compassionate person, who enjoys reading, listening to music and meeting people. She also has a keen interest in nature, travelling and exploring other cultures.

Denise is an accomplished Auditor, Entrepreneur, Professional Certified Business and Life Coach, and an award-winning author. She is also passionate about serving others and extends her outreach within her community through her feeding ministry that helps the indigent.

In addition, Denise also offers services through which she empowers others to overcome challenges and adversities; thus, supporting them on their journey as they rebuild lives of purpose and success. Denise personal and professional coaching services and can be reached at dhyltona@yahoo.com.

www.ingramcontent.com/pod-product-compliance
Lightning Source LLC
Chambersburg PA
CBHW032130090426
42743CB00007B/547